HUNTING MEN

ZACK,

   I APPRECIATE YOUR INTREST
IN MY BOOK.

   BEST WISHES

HUNTING MEN

The Career of an Oregon State Police Detective

MIKE DAVIS

abbott press®

A DIVISION OF WRITER'S DIGEST

Abbott Press books may be ordered through booksellers or by contacting:

Abbott Press
1663 Liberty Drive
Bloomington, IN 47403
www.abbottpress.com
Phone: 1-866-697-5310

ISBN: 978-1-4582-1600-7 (sc)
ISBN: 978-1-4582-1602-1 (hc)
ISBN: 978-1-4582-1601-4 (e)

Library of Congress Control Number: 2014909090

Printed in the United States of America.

Abbott Press rev. date: 06/05/14

CONTENTS

A Tribute to a Cop's Wife

To Shari, my loving wife
Shari, I'm sure you've heard at times during our married life,
From those who ask. Aren't you proud to be a detective's wife?
But Shari let me say this: It's you I'm proud of, and they would be too,
If only they could see what it takes to be one
and what she had to go through.
To be a lawman is no easy task, to do what we have to do.
But it's a much harder job to be his wife, and
it takes someone special like you.
And I know God chose you to be with me in this life,
Because He knew you had the qualities and strength to be a cop's wife.
Some may say I have courage and I'm a hero and that sort of thing:
And when I hear it, this thought to my mind it always brings:
It's you Shari, you're the courage behind the man's badge, don't you see:
And it's you Shari who is the real hero, not me.
And I know you get lonely and frustrated at
times and wonder if it's worth it all:
But if you ever left me, this brave, coura-
geous "hero" would be no man at all.
And I know you worry about the temptations I face on the street,
Of the women of the night and girls that I meet,
But let me tell you this, Shari, and you listen good:
There's nobody on this earth that could re-
place you, they certainly never could.
And I know there are times when I go to
work and you kiss me goodbye,
That you must worry and wonder if this is
the day I've been chosen to die.
And Shari if that should ever happen and someday come true,
Remember Shari, my very last thoughts on earth will be of you.

All my love, your husband,
Mike Davis, Detective
Oregon State Police—Criminal Division
Pendleton, Oregon
Retired, August 1, 2004

PROLOGUE

F<small>RIENDS AND FAMILY HAVE</small> told me for years I should write a book but I dismissed the idea. I thought no one would be interested in what I did for a living. Last year a friend of mine, Mike Lynch gave me a book written by Joe Schaub, a retired Oregon State Police fish and game officer whom I had known. As I walked away, Mike said, "You should write a book." I read the book, and it reminded me of how unique a career in law enforcement is.

The stories I will relate to you are true. I will change the names of most of the characters and culprits involved in these events to either save them embarrassment or protect their reputations.

If my old partners knew I was at a computer writing down some of the things we did over our career, they would not sleep well at night. Not that what we did was illegal; it was simply a different time, and things were done differently. Sleep tight my brothers; you are safe with me.

I have never shared most of these stories, since they did not seem important at the time. However, to get an idea of what shaped my career and attitude you need to know some background.

I will give you the Readers Digest version of my career in law enforcement. I hope to entertain you with some adventures, not educate you with any useful information. The only thing you may learn is how and why cops retire with similar attitudes.

I want to thank my kids Jason and Tiffany who put up with a hard ass father who had seen a lot of kids go bad, so I over reacted a lot. Jason is a Lt. Colonel in the Air Force and Tiffany is a Registered Nurse. I could not be any prouder of their accomplishments and that they are good citizens, thanks to their mom.

INTRODUCTION

I HAVE BEEN OUT of law enforcement for ten years. I thought it was time for my family and civilian friends to know what I did for a living. My wife did not know much more than an outsider, because I wanted to protect my family from the world I worked in. I tried never to bring the job home; if I had to vent I vented to other cops or a couple of very close friends. She did know the dangers were real, and I know she worried constantly.

Near the end of my career a SWAT commander had a good idea. We brought the families in for a week of training. It gave the families some piece of mind knowing we were constantly training and preparing for the worst. During one phase of training, the counter-snipers snuck up to within a few yards of our families who were in stadium seats. It seems like a small thing, but it made them realize we were good at what we did. My wife told someone just the other day how I had snuck up on them at a training exercise, so I know it made an impression. There were times when I was involved in a shooting or a partner was killed, my wife did not know if I was safe or not, for those times I am truly sorry.

My journey through twenty-eight years of law enforcement experiences shaped my life and career. I was a tough athletic kid who grew up in

Eastern Oregon. The worst thing I did growing up was get into fights. I was an Eagle Scout, I enjoyed the outdoors. I wrestled in High School, I was recruited to wrestle at the University of Oregon and I wrestled on the All Marine Team.

I rode dirt bikes and was continually attempting to avoid the Oregon State Police officers in our area. I outran most of my pursuers on my dirt bike, but was stopped several times in the family car. The few tickets I got were deserved and I was warned most of the time. The professional demeanor of the Oregon State Police impressed me and I decided that before I left High School I wanted to join the Oregon State Police.

In 1974 I got married and we moved to Eugene where I was working as an armed security officer at Lumber Mills and Constructions Companies while going to college. This was the first time I had someone shooting near me out of anger. A lumber mill had lain off employees during the recession and people were angry. As I was making my rounds at the lumber mill, a pickup pulled in and started shooting into the area where I was standing. I could hear the bullets as they passed by, it was exciting for a twenty-year old.

Within a month of the shooting incident the security company I was working for lost several contracts and I lost my job. That day I went to the Oregon State Police office to ask what I could do to assure I would get hired when I turned twenty-one, I was told to join the Marine Corps. I went to the recruiter took the test and joined the Marine Corps that day, it was one of the best decisions I ever made.

After getting out of the Marine Corps early I assumed I was going to the Academy right away. I drove directly from Camp Pendleton to Salem Oregon and was told I would not be in the upcoming class, but I would be hired in the fall. There was no reason given, I later found out that they were running their first class of women recruits, I believed they were the Gemini class. I will not elaborate on the success of that program.

I was very disappointed I wasn't hired especially since I had a new baby boy and a daughter on the way. After lying about my qualifications and using my veteran's preference points I was hired by the Forest Service as a Sawyer and part time cat operator.

I started out as every young police officer does. I am sure the reasons to go into law enforcement varied. I have no idea why the rest of my brothers in law enforcement wanted to be a police officer, but I hated bad guys. I had no illusions that I was doing the public good, I just wanted to arrest bad guys. Through my career I learned that not all the people I arrested were bad people some were people who made bad decisions. Don't misunderstand I did arrested some very bad people too.

When I left the Marine Corps as a corporal I was making $350 a month. The state police was starting me out at $700 a month, and due to the early out program, the military was kicking in $150 a month until I got off recruit status—I thought I was rich.

Before I go any farther I need to thank the Oregon State Police for allowing me to be part of a great organization. I would never have had the opportunities I had in my career without the department's trust in me. I will make some observations along the way that may seem like I am bashing the Oregon State Police, nothing could be farther from the truth.

You can go into any organization and find idiots either working with you or in charge at some level. If I mention an incident where one of those idiots did or said something stupid there are a hundred good guys making good decisions all around him. The same goes for other agencies I will mention along the way.

At one point I wrote a letter to the one of the new governor's explaining why he should remove the superintendent of the Oregon State Police. New governors have the option of removing department heads upon taking office. The governor chose to forward my letter to the superintendent. That was ok there was nothing in the letter I would not have said directly to the superintendent.

However, headquarters hacked my computer and the document was frozen for about two weeks while they tried to figure out if they could do anything to me. I think they searched every corner of that computer, I could see the curser moving all over the place when the screen was on. I always felt you should speak your mind. I did my job, but more importantly I covered my ass at all times. I may have been one of those idiots.

I moved out of State upon retirement, I thought it would be nice to get a fresh start where people did not know what I did for a living. The worst thing to tell a civilian was that you were a state police officer. The Oregon State Police is not a highway patrol; the assignments vary greatly. Most people think we all chased taillights and gave honest hard working people a bad time.

If you tell a person at a party that you were in law enforcement, you can bet that you will hear about a speeding ticket they received. The last speeding ticket I wrote was in the early 1980s.

Do not misunderstand or feel I am bashing on anyone who works uniformed patrol his or her whole career. I have the upmost respect for this job choice; but I tried it, and I knew it was not for me. When you are out there at night with no backup for fifty miles or more; it takes a great deal of courage to stop carloads of potentially armed people. The work is hard on officers and their families. I want to thank them for their sacrifice and service.

It's difficult for people to understand the variety of assignments involved with the Oregon State Police. I will attempt to paint a picture of some of these jobs. Everyone starts out as a patrol officer. This does not mean that he only writes speeding tickets. As a young patrol officer I worked cases involving fish and game, burglaries, arsons, thefts, death investigations, domestic violence, drug cases, forgeries, as well as the standard patrol duties. As a patrol officer (trooper) you are allowed to follow up on cases to a certain point. However, if you are working graveyard, you likely can't make the contacts necessary to complete a case. At that point there may be a decision to hand it off to detectives, and *that* was my passion.

LIFE WITH A COACH

EVERYTHING YOU EXPERIENCE IN your career and life transforms you into who you ultimately become and how you react to similar experiences in the future.

In 1977 I started my career with the Oregon State Police (OSP) in Eugene. When OSP assigns coaches at the academy, it is with great anticipation. All of the state police officers I knew were intimidating. When my coach, Don, was introduced, I was shocked. Here was this skinny guy wearing horn-rimmed glasses and smoking a cigarette. He looked like a schoolteacher. In fact he had been a firefighter for several years, and the Oregon State Police had hired him when he was forty years old. We were oil and water. I wanted a young, badass coach who wanted to tear up the world; instead I got Don. As it turned out, Don was the best coach I could have asked for. He was mature and grounded. The verdict was still out on me.

My inexperience got Don into his first fight. I stopped what I thought was a decent guy, who told me he did not have his license with him, so I gave him a warning. Don asked when I got back to the car if I had checked his drivers status. I had not, and of course his driving privileges were suspended for a felony so he should have gone to jail. I found him a short time later at home. I guess he thought once he was home he was

1

safe. Needless to say he did not go to jail willingly. Don was not happy with me. He was smooth and had always been able to talk guys into the car. This was unfortunately not Don's last fight while I was with him.

Don suggested I write the office average of seven tickets per day and then go do police work. It was easy to get seven tickets in a couple of hours in an area like Eugene. By profiling drivers I could get two or three uninsured motorists a day without trying, then I could head off the freeway for some police work. I primarily worked east of Eugene up Highway 58 near Dexter and Lowell. I seemed to run into a lot of people I could take to jail.

Don taught me to interview suspects regarding criminal investigations. We got most of our suspects to confess. We had a criminal division in Eugene that handled the more complicated cases, but we were allowed to follow up on our own cases. I realized early on that I could not write speeding tickets to "mom and pop" my whole career. The department soured me on writing speeding tickets when the federal government forced us to enforce fuel conservation speeds.

During your recruit time, you ride a week with the detectives and a week with the fish and wildlife officers. On the first day with the fish and wildlife officer, we were driving out through the woods when he asked me how good I was with my revolver. I told him I was a good shot. He said, "Good. You have any bucks on the right. I'll take the ones on the left." At first I thought it was a test, but he was serious. Back then the fish and wildlife officers could shoot a deer, go off duty to process the deer, and then go back on duty. At first glance it seemed like the dream job.

After you have been with your coach for a couple months, you are thrown out on your own. The supervisors don't really trust you at this point, so you can only work days. I don't think they are protecting you from the bad guys; there are just more supervisors around to chew your ass during the day.

To start our day out right the other recruit, Ron Wampole, and I found out we could go through the file where OSP kept arrest warrants and search for suspects with outstanding warrants. We selected warrants with a bail higher than $5,000, so they could not pay and we could take them to jail.

The first time we went out with an arrest warrant, the guy opened the door before he realized Ron and I were there. When he saw us, he threw the door at us and ran into the house. We both hit him at the same time sending us all over a couch, we were hooked

I went to advanced recruit school and took a final physical fitness test; my old recruit school roommate and former marine, Cal, and I had a perfect score on the fitness test, so the superintendent came over to congratulate us on our performance and asked what we thought of the department. I told him that the fuel conservation speed enforcement on the freeway was isolating us from the citizens. While working the rural areas around Eugene, local residents were thanking me for patrolling their area. I told him I had been thirty miles out in the country when the dispatcher called me back to work Interstate 5. Six patrol cars were lined up in front of a supervisor who was calling out speeds five miles per hour over the speed limit. The superintendent thanked me for my opinion and walked away. I felt great the boss had recognized me and listened to what I had to say.

About a week later I was called into the station commander's, Ernie's, office. He proceeded to rip me a new one, asking if I was unhappy working the road and whether I wanted to work fish and wildlife or what. I said I had thought about it but had decided that the Fish and Wildlife Division was too chicken shit for me.

Ernie finally realized I had no idea why I was called into his office. Ernie said the superintendent told him that I had criticized the speed enforcement program on the freeway. I said that was true. Ernie said, "I don't tell the superintendent what I think." He said the

3

speed enforcement on the freeway was the superintendent's idea, and I had infuriated him. Another lesson learned is to keep your mouth shut, even when asked your opinion. As a recruit I could be fired for cause, as there were no unions or associations to offer protection at that time.

HIGH-SPEED ADVENTURES

High-speed chases were common; even my mild-mannered coach could stand on a gas pedal. The first week with Don we were traveling south on I-5; I had my head down and was writing in my notebook, when we passed a car on the side of road. I started to ask Don if we were going to check the vehicle when I realized we were in the fast lane traveling at 130 miles per hour. The car was probably traveling at sixty-five, so at a glance it looked like it was standing still.

No wonder I drove so fast on patrol—I had a good teacher! If you went with the flow of traffic you looked at the same vehicles all the time, so it was necessary to go faster than the flow. I know the general public did not like you following them for miles from place to place, so everyone should have been happy that we were passing them. However you had the occasional asshole citizen who wanted to turn you in or make a citizen's arrest for speeding. I nipped that in the bud. If someone pulled in behind me and tried to follow, I would do a short frontal pace, pull over, and give them a ticket. We paced cars from the rear all the time it should have been no big deal pacing them from the front. As time passed the department did not like this practice.

After Don let me drive, I took full advantage of the high-speed driving. He told me I would crash a car someday. The only wreck I was in was when another patrol car hit me. The 1977 Pontiacs had a tendency of dying if you were at high speed and dynamited the brakes.

I came into an interchange at high speed and slammed on the brakes before the turn, and my car died. I had another marked unit following me, chasing the same call. I pulled onto the shoulder and coasted to a stop. It was dark and the other unit followed my taillights off the road hitting me from the rear.

//

I blew out a tire at over a hundred miles per hour. I had been dispatched to a man with a gun at the Oak Grove Rest Area. I was traveling at 135 miles per hour and had just slowed a bit to pass a truck in the Goshen curves south of Eugene, when the right rear tire blew. I held onto the wheel and let off the gas. I could see the trucker lock up his brakes. I was throwing rubber and molding all over the place. It took about a mile to stop, and I used both lanes of the freeway. I changed the tire as fast as I could but it was so hot I could barely touch it. It took me a while to get there, and I never did find a man with a gun.

//

I was chasing a guy on the freeway, when he crossed the median into oncoming traffic and turned out his headlight. Department policy said we should not chase someone on the wrong side of the freeway, but I knew oncoming traffic would not see him and someone would get killed. I crossed over behind him with my lights on high beam and overheads activated.

We were both traveling in excess of a hundred miles per hour. We came to a long downhill run where I knew I could pass him, so I did. That was when I realized I had made a huge mistake. The suspect started trying to run up on me and clip my bumper in an attempt to spin me out. About the second pass at my bumper I sped up and he lost control.

He shot over the median and crashed into the guard rail on the far side of the freeway. By the time I got to him other patrol cars involved in the pursuit had already begun to "educate" the suspect. All I was left with was an adrenaline rush.

//

Some high speed chases were not people attempting to elude us. I was assigned patrol duties west of Pendleton on I-84; the traffic was light, and it was a sunny day. I was watching traffic from off the freeway, when I saw a Ferrari traveling at high speed. It took me about ten miles to catch up with the car. I was able to pace the driver for about two miles and activated my overheads. After about a mile I pulled alongside him and got his attention. We were traveling between ninety-five to one hundred miles per hour.

I contacted the owner of the Ferrari and asked if he knew how fast he was going. He acknowledged that he did, he said he had just bought the car and was taking it for a spin. I took his information and handed him back his driver's license. I told him to have a nice day. He looked at me in astonishment expecting a ticket. I told him the next trooper may not be such a fan. He was diving in a safe manner, and the car was more than capable of handling such speeds. I sped everywhere I went, so I had a bit of a moral dilemma when it came to writing speeding tickets.

My dad loved to drive fast. He had raced cars at the Orange County speedway in California before he went to Korea. The family cars he bought were capable of high speeds. One time Dad and I were in an Olds Cutlass with a 454, headed to Portland on I-84 when I was a kid. The freeway was posted with a basic speed of seventy-five miles per hour, which meant it was a "suggested" speed. We were traveling somewhere north of one hundred miles per hour near Arlington, Oregon. A trooper stopped us and asked my dad if he knew how fast he was going. My dad said he did. The trooper walked around the car looked

7

at the tires and told my dad to have a nice day, and then handed him back his driver's license.

I had a similar experience while driving back from a wrestling tournament with a carload of wrestlers. I was on I-84 near Hood River traveling over ninety miles per hour when a trooper stopped me. He asked what we were doing. I told him we were headed home from a wrestling tournament. He told me to take it easy and drove off.

I-84 was designed for high speed driving. The only reason we have a posted speed of sixty-five miles per hour is that the federal government threatened to take away funding if the Oregon State Police did not enforce a fuel conservation speed. This is also why I had a soft spot for speeders.

//

One sunny afternoon I saw a Corvette on the other side of the freeway traveling at an extremely high rate of speed. I cut across the median and took chase. I was starting to lose ground when I saw a cloud of dust and trucks pulling over. I pulled up in time to the Corvette rolling; both people had been ejected. As far as I could tell both the driver and passenger were dead, when the driver started convulsing.

I called Life Flight, who picked up the driver and was able to save him. A witness said he was in the right lane when the Corvette passed and changed lanes too hard. The driver lost control and spun around in the freeway. The Corvette ended up nose to nose with the witness going backward at an excessive speed. The Corvette started fish tailing, lost control, and rolled in the median numerous times. I never did find out why they were going so fast.

//

I quit chasing motorcycles early on in my career. If I could get close enough to identify their gear and get a license plate number, I let them go and called ahead. I had kids on motorcycles blow stop lights at over a hundred miles per hour while I was chasing them. I cited several at home at a later date.

//

While I was working narcotics, the OSP purchased pursuit vehicles. They bought some Camaros and Mustangs. One of the troopers let me take his car for a spin; I reached 130 miles per hour by the end of the off ramp. By the time I got up around 150 mph, the car felt like I was driving a boat; it was light as a feather. I shut it down and took it back. It was fun but I had had enough.

//

I pursued a car load of juveniles in a stolen car, and after a few miles they decided to pull over. By the time I got them all out of the car I had six teenagers on the pavement. A concerned motorist stopped and asked if there was anything he could do. I told him he could watch the kids while I called in—we did not yet have portable radios. I unloaded the shotgun, racked the action, and handed it to him. In my gruffest voice I told him to shoot anyone who moved, then I whispered to him that if they run let them go. I went back to my patrol car and called for assistance.

DEALING WITH WOMEN

I HAD A LEARNING curve when it came to women. I got married young, and I had not been around many nasty or aggressive woman.

Don and I did not get a lot of drunk drivers; some I even let go. One night I stopped a good-looking, well-endowed ski bunny coming off the mountain from a day of skiing. As it happened, I had stopped her about a block from her house. After talking to her for a while and giving her some tests, she invited me to her place after I got off work. She said she would leave her door unlocked, while she was rubbing up and down me like an alley cat. I was so flustered I told her to take it easy going home and walked back to the patrol car. As she drove off Don asked if she was drunk I told him yes I believe she was.

Sexual advances were not uncommon, at least when I was young. One time while working with Don we stopped two cars. Don did not lock his door and was taking to the driver of the car behind us. I was running the driving status of a young lady, when she walked back, opened the passenger door, and crawled over the console. She put her arms around my neck telling me that she would do "anything" to get out of the ticket. As I looked over her shoulder Don walked up looked in and was shaking his head.

These scenarios were not uncommon, especially with drunken women. First of all you had caught them in a vulnerable position; they knew they were in trouble, and they were under the influence of alcohol.

One woman stripped down naked in the back of my patrol car, while I was giving dispatch a blow-by-blow account. I'm sure people in scanner land were very amused. It's uncomfortable marching a naked woman into the jail. As a side note, it's easier for women to slip off handcuffs due to the size of their hands compared to their wrists. I had women slip their cuffs several times during my career.

Another approach was for women to pull their tops down (tube tops were popular) or their skirts up when you walked up to the car. Every gal who showed me her tits or her crotch got a ticket. I assumed that it had worked several times before, and she had probably earned this ticket. When you walked back up, and they realized they were getting a ticket anyway, the contact would normally take a nasty turn.

Often women I took to jail invited me you back to their homes. I think some misunderstood the fact that you were just treating them with respect.

Trespassing calls along the river in the summer were common. These cases were normally naked college girls sunning themselves. This soon became a dreaded task. No one should have seen most of these gals naked. Remember it was the late seventies, and I was in Eugene.

I could not count the times we arrested naked women who were combative or overly friendly, while we were executing search warrants early in the morning. I remember one of the women we told to get dressed came out wearing a leather micro miniskirt and, as it turned out, no panties. While interviewing her, she kept spreading her legs.

A woman who I had arrested several times came by the office one day to give me some information. I knew her history very well, she was extremely attractive and well endowed. My partners did not know her but were extremely interested in being in the area and wanted an introduction. While I was talking to her I wrote this short note: "She has AIDS and hepatitis," and I handed it to one of my partners who passed it around the room. You should have seen the expression on their faces.

We were as nice to people as they were to us. A lot of women were in very abusive situations and had never been treated well. Some women mistakenly believed that being treated with respect was some type of sexual advance, or that we expected sex for treating them with respect. That is why we had a rule; no one meets a female informant alone.

You can't blame the high divorce rate of police officers on women willing to work off tickets or arrests, but if a guy was not happy at home, you can see how it would be easy to stray. I have known more than one police officer who took advantage of these situations and lost his job.

ATTITUDE CHANGE

I THOUGHT THAT WHEN I put the uniform on I would earn some measure of respect just because I was a state trooper. Growing up in Eastern Oregon, I did not know anyone who would have targeted police officers or challenge their authority. So I was somewhat taken back by the way some people treated me, when I would contact them. It never crossed my mind that people would want to kill me because I was a trooper. I saw all the officer shooting videos in recruit school, but it does not sink in until you have a come-to-Jesus moment.

Your first two years are critical. When I was hired, most police officers killed had less than two years of service. One night I was on the way back to the state police office in Eugene from the jail. I saw a guy stuck on the curb near the university. As I pulled up I saw a middle aged Black male in a three-piece suit. He was crying and had a pronounced limp. As I contacted him he was polite and courteous. After talking with him and administering some sobriety tests, I decided to arrest him for driving while intoxicated.

Since he had not been any trouble I decided to cuff him in front, I patted him down and went to his car to turn it off. As I leaned into the car he came up behind me and put his hand on my back feeling my vest. I reached back and told him to step back and pushed him slightly as he was near my weapon. At the same time I saw some headlights coming up behind us. As I looked up the suspect had a buck knife in both hands up over his head, and I was trapped in the doorway. Both of us realized it was another patrol car at the same time. As I drew my weapon he threw the knife on the ground, put his hands in the air, turned his back to me, and walked toward the patrol car.

As I walked up to him he stopped crying and asked how old I was. I said twenty-four. He looked me square in the eye and said if you were working in LA, you would not live to see twenty-five. That was a defining moment in my life as a police officer. He told me he was a gang member from Los Angeles who had had his leg shot off in a gun fight. He was not wanted and had not committed a serious crime. He had no reason for attempting to stab me, other than I was a police officer. I realized right then that I was not a very good judge of character. I had given people the benefit of the doubt until that moment. From that point on I cuffed everybody I arrested behind their back even if I had to fight them to get the cuffs on.

//

Even though Eugene and Springfield had large police departments, they did not work outside the city limits unless it was an emergency. On graveyard it was not uncommon for me to be the only trooper working in Lane County. About a month after the incident with the drunk driver who wanted to kill me, I was dispatched to assist a deputy near Lowell with a dispute. As I arrived I saw a person in custody in the back of the deputy's patrol car. He told me that the suspect's brother had threatened to shoot him for arresting the suspect.

There was a full moon as I looked toward the woods I saw a person with a rifle silhouetted against light colored clothing. I ran toward the person and cut them off. As I approached him he turned and came at me with the rifle hollering; the rifle was not pointed at me. He said he was going to kill the deputy for arresting his brother. He was about sixteen years old. I was forced to knock him out to get the rifle from him. That was another lesson learned: people may not know you but they are willing to kill you, if you are in their way.

//

Because I was young and aggressive, I was placed on graveyard for over a year. I got very good at arresting drunk drivers. I was arresting around three hundred a year, which meant I was dealing with a lot more aggressive people and people not wanting to go to jail. The amount of fights or scuffles skyrocketed over time. Even a pleasant drunk who did not want to get handcuffed could get aggressive. I had several drunks say they would get into the car, but they would not let me handcuff them. I'd just smile, because I knew they were getting cuffed even if it meant I would have to fight them.

//

Our station commander, Ernie, was a cop's cop. If you got into a fight on patrol, he wanted to hear all the details—not so he could chastise you, but because he wanted to tell you a war story of his own. I don't know how many unconscious guys he left alongside the road, but I got the impression it was more than a few.

After having Ernie as a station commander, I thought that station commanders were there to protect us—an impression that would haunt me down the road. I watched a guy come into the office to complain about a trooper, and after a couple of insults Ernie threw him out of the office. As he threw him toward the door, the guy's face hit the door jam. I knew as long as I was right, Ernie would defend me.

//

We had a trooper who had gotten in a fight with a drunk. The drunk got away from him, got back into the car, and then led him on a

15

high-speed chase. The department charged the trooper with Shrinking in the Face of Danger. What a jacket to hang on a guy! He did not appear to be the kind of guy to run from a fight—he just was not very tough. He was a nice guy who did not fit in with the other ruffians in the office. What was the lesson? Don't lose a fight and do not back down, or you will be branded as a coward.

//

One night while taking a drunk to jail, I went into the holding area of the old Lane County Jail. As I got inside I could smell smoke and hear yelling. I put my gun in the locker and was let into the booking area. I was told there was a riot and that the prisoners were lighting mattresses on fire and flooding the place.

It was total chaos. I told them to let the drunk and me out, and I would take him home. I was told they needed help to control the inmates. I was issued a Louisville Slugger and sent into the jail. There was smoke in the air and a couple of inches of water on the floor.

Inmates were coming at me with socks filled with porcelain from sinks they had smashed. They were swinging their socks over their heads like medieval weapons. I was ducking and hitting inmates with the baseball bat, until I worked my way to the back of the isolation area. After witnessing what was happening to their fellow inmates who did not follow instructions some inmates gave up and came out peacefully. About fifteen inmates went to the hospital and were in need of medical attention.

//

My first criminal case was a daytime burglary near a school. One of the items taken was a collection of fifty-cent pieces. I found small footprints at the scene, so I went to the school and found out a couple of boys were using fifty-cent pieces to purchase items at school. I got more enjoyment working criminal cases than I ever did stopping cars. I'm not berating what patrol officers do every day or the dangers of walking up on the unknown, but I really wanted to work plainclothes.

//

Since I had been arresting a few people snagging salmon on the McKenzie River, the fish and game officers let me do some undercover work off duty. I would go to local snagging areas and watch for snagging, drug use, and people throwing down poles when the game guys walked up. I would watch the crowd for an hour or two, and then the game guys would roll in. It was my first taste of undercover work and I loved it.

//

I liked nontraditional traffic enforcement. I had several local businesses that would send out illegal equipment with employees. Some of the owners refused to fix the equipment, even after I had warned them. I did not want to cite the employee, so I went after the owners for Allowing Unlawful Operation of a Vehicle.

One particular operation was continually violating the law, so I contacted the owner at his place of business. Things got ugly the minute I arrived and told the owner why I was there. He was about 6'4" and very loud; he refused to take a ticket for a violation his employees had committed. He attempted to get away from me by going into the office. As he turned I was able to jump high enough to get him in a choke hold so I could pull him off his feet to the ground. His wife and employees started to move in to assist the owner. After I ordered them to back off, his wife insisted he had heart trouble, so I sat him on the ground and told him if he tried to get up I would knock him back down. He stayed there and took the ticket.

After I left the business I got a call to come to the office. I was told that there had been a complaint and the owner was on the way to the hospital with heart problems. I went in and told Ernie what had happened. He told me that the criminal sergeant and a detective were going to the hospital to interview the owner of the business.

About an hour later the detectives came back and said the family wanted to know if I wanted to be a pallbearer; the owner had died before they arrived. Ernie told me to do a report on the incident. About an hour later Ernie and the detectives came in and told me that the owner had hyperventilated. They laughed about it for days. Police humor you got to love it.

//

One night I arrested a drunk on a raised section of I-105 on the west side of Eugene. While I was placing him in the back of the patrol car, one of his drunken buddies got into his car and drove off. I caught up to him and got him stopped. He was mad because he said I told him he could drive. I told him he was under arrest for DUI, and the fight was on. It was raining hard as usual. During the fight I went to kick him in the groin, my feet went out from under me, and I landed on my back. I waited for the suspect to jump on me—since I was a wrestler I preferred to fight on the ground, but instead he took off running.

It was over a mile before the freeway dropped down to level ground, and it was at least a thirty-foot drop. I started after him and caught him once. I hit the bridge with my fist during the struggle, and he took off again. The boots and vest were getting heavy, and I started losing ground to him.

I flagged down an old man and his wife they drove me ahead of the suspect cutting him off. When he saw me coming he jumped off the bridge. He fell into some wet grass and flopped around like a fish out of water. The old folks drove me around to him and called an ambulance to transport him to the hospital.

I got back to my patrol car, which was still there running with the lights on. My suspect was standing next to the patrol car. His girlfriend had let him out of the patrol car. He apologized for his friend's behavior. Again, a lesson was learned: don't leave your car unattended. It could have easily been stolen. I'm glad I had witnesses to the jumper. I still have guys giving me a bad time about throwing the guy off the bridge.

//

About the same time as the bridge incident I was working I-205, when I saw a car chasing another car without headlights. I followed them off the freeway and into a residential area. The lead vehicle stopped at a house, and a woman got out. She was being chased by a guy in the second car.

I caught him as he caught her. I knocked him onto his back and landed on his chest. He reached up and grabbed me by the family jewels. I beat the guy until he released his grip. While I was cuffing him, he was still fighting and telling me how many Free Souls (a biker group) were in Eugene and how they would take care of me.

On the way to jail he threatened to burn my kids up on the way to school. I was forced to stop the patrol car and continue his education. I met the past president of the Free Souls and would occasionally meet with him while on patrol. He told me that the Free Souls had worked this guy over after he got out of jail—they did not want trouble from the cops. They were at war with the Gypsy Jokers in Portland, Oregon.

//

One night I stopped a college student and noticed he was attempting to hide a second driver's license as he dug through his wallet. I took the license and found he had a forged document. After quizzing him for a while, I learned that some of the engineering students at the university had made a scale model of a driver's license. They could stand in the location of the picture take a snap shot and shrink it down to the size of a driver's license. They had done a great job. I was impressed with the quality of the work.

I convinced him to take me to the dorms so I could seize the template. While I was collecting evidence, I saw a bright light coming from a closet. I found a marijuana "grow" in the closet; it was a bad night for the kid and his roommate. I collected several more driver's licenses from other students. These were the type of case I wanted to work. A routine traffic stop turned into a criminal case.

//

There were funny drunks too. I saw a guy stuck in the loose gravel on a freeway interchange. The car was buried to the frame and the tires were spinning. He was focused straight ahead and thought he was driving. I scared him to death when I banged on the window.

//

I was working on I-5 near Eugene and stopped a carload of college-aged guys and what appeared to be a homely woman in the passenger seat. Everyone in the vehicle seemed nervous; none of them had a story that made any sense. After I had gotten identification from the driver I realized the he was not intoxicated, so I turned my attention to what I realized must be a prostitute. While she was digging for more iden-tification from a purse I saw several pill bottles and what appeared to be some illegal drugs. I asked what the drugs were for. I was told that they were hormone pills and medication. She said, "I am a transvestite."

You should have seen the look on the young men's faces. Apparently there was a little false advertisement going on when they picked up the prostitute. I could barely contain myself. Then one of the boys said, "Take her with you." I told them, "You caught it you clean it!"

I really don't know what happened after I turned them loose, but I would guess they dropped off their prize where they found it.

//

I had a bad experience with the legal system in Eugene. I stopped a local business man for erratic driving on I-5; he was a very big man. When I contacted him he refused to get out of the car. I had seen enough to arrest him for drunk driving, so I pried him out of the car. I had arm-barred his left arm and put him against his vehicle.

There was a pit bull in the car. While I was looking at the dog, the suspect started falling to the right and hit the pavement with his right cheek. He never attempted to break his fall with his free arm. Since he was so much bigger than I was, I immediately jumped on him and got him handcuffed, which was no easy task due to the size of his wrists.

When we got to the jail he started saying, "Don't hit me any more officer." He used the photos of his bloody cheek and red wrists to sue me. The state decided it was cheaper to pay him off than to fight the charges, and they dropped the DUII arrest. That left a very bad taste in my mouth; the liberal system in Eugene was not law enforcement friendly.

//

I stopped a businessman speeding on the freeway. For me to stop anybody for speeding, he had to have been flying. He was rude from the beginning, which I always enjoyed. It just made writing a ticket easier. I handed him the ticket, told him to have a nice day, and started to leave.

He wadded up the ticket and threw it at me. I tossed him onto the hood of my patrol car and cuffed him. Then away we went to the courthouse. We were probably twenty miles from Eugene. Court was in session, so I took him directly before a judge.

As I told the judge what had happened, my suspect started hanging his head nodding in agreement. The judge asked my suspect if that was what happened. He said it was. The judge found him guilty and fined him more than the standard bail. As I was leaving, he asked the judge how he was going to get back to his vehicle. The judge looked to me for an answer. I told the judge that I was not a taxi service and walked out of the court room. I have no idea how he got back to his vehicle.

//

I'm going to mention one more speeder. Only because last week I was at an NRA banquet and a woman at the table found out my buddy was a cop. She was asking him why a cop would write a ticket to a woman for speeding when she needed to go to the bathroom. Then she asked him how much over the speed limit she could go. First of all, since he had worked narcotics for the last ten years, he probably did not know. He tried to be polite and say that it is up to the individual officer and that he did not know the circumstances. Trust me; there is not a police officer in the country who has not heard those comments. Get some new material, people. Thank him for his service and the sacrifice his family makes, or shut up and eat your dinner in silence.

Your friend who gets a ticket is probably not telling you the whole story. I will give you an example. I was watching traffic from a rest area north of Eugene when a woman passed me at speeds approaching one hundred miles an hour. I pulled out and paced the woman for a few miles. I activated the overhead lights, and she eventually pulled off the freeway at a truck stop. When I contacted her, she said she had to go to the bathroom, so I let her go inside. She returned and told me she had an emergency and needed to use the restroom. Don't forget the first part of my story: I was in the rest area she had passed a bathroom six miles back on the freeway. Yes, I wrote her a speeding ticket.

//

Headquarters in Salem called and requested that a couple of troopers from each office to come to Salem for a protest that was being conducted at the front steps of the state capitol. I jumped at the opportunity—it was something new. During the briefing we learned that the protesters were trying to get the legislature to legalize marijuana.

The mall area in front of the state capitol was full. We were told to hold our ground and cite anyone who we could see smoking pot from the steps. There were some undercover detectives mingling in the crowd. One of these detectives, Gus, was reported to be a no-nonsense fellow. Before we got started that day, I saw Gus drag a guy out of a car window.

We were escorted through a tunnel with our raid gear (helmets, ax handles, and shields). We did some practicing and staged our gear just inside the doors of the capitol. We walked out to a sea of people. I wrote a couple of tickets to a few people who got too close to the steps with their joints, but I was getting bored.

I saw the fellow who had organized the event smoking a joint about fifty yards into the crowd. I grabbed another trooper and asked him to come with me. I got to the organizer and told him I was going to have to cite him. He made an attempt to get the protesters who were within earshot upset. I looked over his shoulder and saw Gus and another detective watching us, so I knew we were not alone. The organizer and I did a little lighthearted verbal sparring, and the crowd started laughing. This situation could have gotten ugly in a hurry, but a little humor went a long way. I used this to my advantage many times.

There were times when humor was totally inappropriate, but it did not stop me from joking around. I had a bad habit of smirking when I got nervous or was getting my ass chewed by the brass. In those cases it did not work as well for me.

Law enforcement in general is completely misunderstood when it comes to inappropriate laughter. I think sometimes police use laughter to keep from crying. You could drive up to a homicide scene or an officer-involved shooting, and half the guys are laughing and joking around. I think it is a type of defense mechanism that the general public will never understand. The only other profession that relates is medicine; I am talking about doctors and nurses.

I have been in emergency rooms that were a riot. I had a drunk driver who was fighting the nurses and swearing at everyone. A doctor walked in and said, "I think we need to check him for internal bleeding." The doctor had the nurse and me hold him down, while he cut him from the belly button down without anything for the pain. He then shoved a tube into him, sucked around with a bulb, and concluded that he was not bleeding. He smiled at the nurse and me and sewed him back up. I loved that doctor.

ACCEPTANCE

I WAS HIRED IN an era when veteran troopers would not talk to the recruits. A couple of the old guys would not talk to me for over a year. You had to prove yourself. The ice breaker seemed to be athletics. We had some serious jocks in the office. With that came massive amounts of testosterone. We had two college quarterbacks and some 6'6" receivers on our city league, flag football team. We never lost a game. Both quarterbacks could throw over fifty yards, and our big guys could out jump any defensive back.

I played football, softball, and basketball, even though I was a wrestler. They used me to soften up the opposition. Sportsmanship was not a priority on our team. One night we went to play a charity basketball event in a small community in the far end of our patrol area. The local kids started kicking our asses. The next thing I knew, fists were flying on the basketball court. I grabbed my sergeant and tried to separate him from the local kids. At the same time the stands started to empty. I saw one of our guys drop a local guy as he stepped onto the basketball court. Somehow we made it out alive. The next morning as we arrived for work, I expected some fallout over our behavior, but the station commander just shook his head over our antics.

My first state police softball tournament was being held in Klamath Falls, so I headed off for my first trip with the boys. Cigars and beer were the order of the day. One of the guys I was riding with had not talked to me before the trip, but after a few beers he was my best friend. His wife had just left him, and he was having a pity party.

We got to Klamath Falls about dark, when the sergeant and the troops in our car decided we should go to Reno. After grabbing some more beer, away we went. When we got to the boarder I realized the sergeant driving was in no shape to drive, so during a piss break I got behind the wheel. The sergeant was angry that a recruit had replaced him behind the wheel. The guys had to drag him away from me.

We were heading through the back country at over one hundred mph, when the trooper next to me yelled because the guy behind him had grabbed his gold chain and jerked on it. The fight was on. He spun around in the seat, put his foot on the steering wheel for leverage, and started punching the guy. I was barely able to keep the car on the road.

A few miles down the road gunfire erupted. I don't know what they found to shoot at; it was dark out. We realized we were going to run out of gas before we got to Reno. As we passed a tavern we saw a car trailer with several gas cans. We located the owner of the trailer in the tavern; he sold us some gas and we were on our way.

We made it to Reno and had seen the sights for about twenty minutes when one of the guys came running by saying the cops were after him. When we got back to the car we found out he had been looking at some peep show when a guy came up and weenie-wagged him, so he dropped him. It was time to go anyway. We made it back into Klamath Falls in time for the first pitch.

I had graduated, everybody in the office trusted me, and I felt like part of the team. I had no idea police work was going to be this much fun. This was obviously before the days of ethics class.

I had been in Eugene two years and had seen and done more than most troopers in Eastern Oregon would in several years. I had ignored Don's advice to take it easy and stay in the middle of the pack when writing tickets. I was working all night and was in court most of the day. We did not get comp time or overtime like today. I did get straight time I could take off if there were enough troops out. Several times I came in exhausted and asked for the night off; I was told I was the only one out. At this rate I was going to burn myself out, but I could not slow down.

I hated Eugene and the arrogant people I was sent there to protect. I knew I would miss the guys and the activity, but I started sending my paperwork in for a transfer to Eastern Oregon. I finally received approval to move to Pendleton in 1980. The second phase of my career was about to kick off.

TRANSFER

Apparently my reputation had preceded me in Pendleton. The station commander in Pendleton was a stern fellow who continually questioned my approach to law enforcement which caught me off guard, and quite frankly irritated me.

The station commander seemed to questions every drug arrest I made. His big deal was how I had been able to find the drugs. I told him I talked to the suspect and got permission to search, he told me to quit doing that. Since I was within the law and I liked arresting people I chose to ignore him. I was now a trooper and we had a new troopers' association to back me. I only had to obey lawful orders he could not order me to not do my job. He was not the last station commander who tried to give me an unlawful order that I was forced to ignore.

As you can tell I occasionally went out of my way to press supervisor's buttons, because I enjoyed it. One evening I was headed out on patrol and the station commander asked me to do something (I really don't remember what it was, because it was not important). Instead of saying ok and leaving, I stopped and said " no I don't think I will". He instantly got infuriated and banged on the counter yelling something like, well then I'm ordering you to do it. I smiled and said that's all I wanted to hear. He knew he had been had, I just wanted to see him loose it and he had. He walked off shaking his head.

My first year in Pendleton I made about fifty DUI arrests even thought it was a lot fewer than I was getting in Eugene it was a lot for the area. I was also going to court in Eugene so often I got a Christmas card from the gals at the motel I was staying at.

Along with the arrests came a few scuffles. I'm sure the fact that I was in more altercations that many of the other troopers it made more work for the station commander. To his credit I did see him chest bump a guy out of the office that was giving me a bad time, I think he felt that was his job.

I may have gotten off on the wrong foot with the supervisors in the office. I took officer safety very seriously. In Pendleton we were occasionally assigned dispatch duty at night. One morning after night shift, one of the sergeants came in and asked why I had not cleaned the office or emptied the trash. I told him that it was not my job; my job was to answer the phones and radio. I told him I would not leave the office to dump the trash—I could miss a call for assistance. He let me know it was an order from the district captain. I told him I would not dump the trash.

The next morning the same sergeant walked in with a cigar, set it on the corner of a desk, and left the room. I walked over put it out and threw it in the trash. A few minutes later the station commander walked into the front office—about the same time the sergeant came back in. The sergeant looked around the room and could not find his cigar. He asked where his cigar was. I told him I was cleaning the office and had thrown it away. He was pissed off but what could he say; the station commander got a chuckle out of it. Cleaning the office was never mentioned to me again.

To highlight my point on dispatching and officer safety, I was working the desk one night when a lady's voice came on the radio and said that a trooper had just been hit by a truck. I got her location then she apparently started changing channels, and I lost contact with her. I dispatched a trooper to that location and found that a truck had caught her door, slamming it into the trooper who was launched over her hood into the ditch. Had I been off emptying the trash I would have missed the call. The trooper recovered from his injuries.

I never said I was easy to supervise, but I always treated people the way they treated me. I called the same supervisor Chicken Shit for picking on a trooper who would not stand up for himself. I got called into the station commander's office for an ass chewing regarding my insubordinate behavior.

I told the station commander that I had a notebook full of troubling information regarding this supervisor. The station commander told me not to keep book on his supervisors and after hearing some of my complaints, he threw me out of the office. The supervisor was in the office for two hours attempting to defend his actions. That was the last time I had an issue with that supervisor.

The lack of officer safety in Pendleton scared the hell out of me especially with the older troops. I would see them arrest one of the good old boys, and without searching him, tell him to get into the patrol car.

This is not a criticism of the individual trooper. They had not experienced the same things I had, even that early in my career. They were professional but they had a slower pace. They took coffee breaks in Pendleton. I rarely took a coffee break in Eugene after I left my coach. I did learn to slow it down a bit, though. Writing four tickets a day and a few warnings, which counted as activities, was plenty. I started taking coffee breaks so I could get to know the officers with whom I was working.

The Pendleton office was not as tight-knit a group as the Eugene office. In Eugene, we did everything together, and we dragged our families along. Pendleton was not like that, and as we got new troopers into the office they seemed even more self-involved. That was probably not a bad thing some of what transpired in Eugene was not good for the public image of the state police. In our defense, back then it was more acceptable to work hard and play harder.

The Pendleton office did have softball teams, fishing trips, and Christmas parties. We did not have the after-work activities, the so-called choir practices. The reality was in Pendleton you could not go into a bar and let your hair down. Everyone in town knew who we were. In Eugene there were so many people you could blend in.

//

If you were assigned east patrol, part of your duties included enforcement on the Umatilla Indian Reservation. The FBI had jurisdiction for felony cases. The state police and sheriff's office handled domestic disputes and traffic infractions.

The first call dispatching me to the reservation was a dispute regarding a hit and run. I arrived at the house and found about thirty people milling around and drinking inside and outside. I asked for the owner of the house. Someone pointed to a tribal elder. I asked him who had hit the vehicle. He never said a word, but simply pointed to the culprit. I asked him if he was driving and had hit the car. He just nodded his head yes, so I took him to jail. No one said a word to me, and I never went to court on the case. They may not have liked me being there, but they respected what I was doing there. That was all I wanted.

//

I arrested an Indian woman for DUI one night near the projects. While I was conducting the investigation, I had a few Indian men in the vicinity that seemed indifferent to my presence or to the fuss this woman was putting up. I ended up dragging the woman back to my patrol car. While I was standing in the door way belting my suspect into the car, I heard a blood curdling scream. I looked up and saw a second Indian female adult on a dead run, headed straight for me. I waited in the door way holding the door until she reached for me. I hit her with the door, causing her to roll into the ditch; the abrupt stop seemed to have taken a little of the fight out of her. The men standing a few yards away seemed neither amused nor concerned about the events they witnessed. I got in my car and drove away.

//

One night I had a concerned citizen stop and ask if I needed help. That was foreign to me. I had never had anyone want to get involved or help in Eugene. I had a suspect in front of my vehicle and was about to take him into custody.

I knew the suspect from a previous contact; he was an Indian kid I knew to be extremely violent, and he had been drinking. The first time I had contacted him a month earlier, he had given me a false name. I later learned who he was and that there was a warrant for his arrest. He had gone into a biker bar in Portland, and the bikers made the mistake of harassing him. He had hurt several of them.

I told the concerned citizen that if I had trouble getting him into custody to use my radio and call for help. I left the citizen by my patrol car and re-contacted the suspect. I called him by his true name and told him there was warrant for his arrest. He tensed up for a bit then followed my commands. I took him into custody without incident. On the way to jail he related the story behind the assault warrant. He said he was minding his own business, and the bikers started pushing him, so he fought, back putting a couple of them in the hospital.

You never want to underestimate people; at first glance this young man looked stout, but what you can't see is there was no quit in him, and he had a lot of heart. I actually had contact with him several times after this incident. I always treated him with respect and he did the same.

//

Like all law enforcement officers, you dreaded the family-beef calls. In Pendleton if things were slow, you could stop by your house to have dinner. One evening I was having dinner, and I got a call about a family beef northwest of Pendleton in the wheat field country about thirty miles from where I was. I heard them dispatch a supervisor who was in Pendleton; I figured he was ahead of me so I stepped on it.

I arrived first and saw tufts of long hair in the yard, where the wife had been dragged around. She came out and told me her husband was drunk and was in the house. I did not see the supervisor, but I was not going to wait. The minute I contacted the husband, the fight was on. We fought across the living room knocking furniture everywhere. I got him in an arm bar but he would not give up. I applied some serious pressure and could feel tendons popping, and he let out a yell. His robe, which was the only thing he had on, was around his neck. He was on his knees, face down. I was glad I was off to one side. He cut loose with a stream of loose diarrhea that shot clear across the room. He must have been on a weeklong drunk.

I mentioned a supervisor who was dispatched at same time I was. He arrived after I had the suspect in the car and I had finished interviewing the wife. I never said a word I just made a mental note.

//

One night on the reservation I chased a driver who was attempting to elude me. The chase ended at a private residence. As I jumped out of the vehicle, the suspect ran toward me, which was new to me. *I* usually had to run *suspects* down. I took out my nightstick and met him at the front of my vehicle. I hit him in both knees and he kept coming. I grabbed him and tossed him over the hood of my patrol car. As soon as he hit the hood, he reached back with his right hand and drew my revolver from the holster. My night stick was still in my right hand. I grabbed the revolver with my left hand. I repeatedly struck the suspect in the head with the night stick, while I re-holstered my revolver. The suspect made it a few feet away before he fell. I ordered him repeatedly to show his hands, which were under him. I hit him on the elbows several times before I realized he was unconscious.

I cuffed him and transported him to the hospital, where I was asked if he had been in a traffic accident. I guess he did not look so good. The nice thing about living in a small community is that you run into the same people over and over. The next time I ran into this fellow all I heard was, "Yes sir," and, "No sir."

Law enforcement officers may not need to have people fear them, but folks need to know what happens if they step over the line. That fellow carried the bandages and scars around for a long time; you can't buy advertising like that.

//

Daren, one of the older troopers in the office, was my tour guide for my first Pendleton Roundup—what an event! It truly revived drinking, fighting, and wild women of the Wild West. Daren was like a UN ambassador for the state police in Pendleton; everyone seemed to know and respect him.

While we were making the rounds, I saw a cowboy whom I had arrested the day before heading right for me through the crowd. I got in my best defensive stance and waited for him. As he got within reach, he extended his hand so I shook hands with the gentleman. He said,

"You probably saved me from making a bigger mistake!" That type of response was something I never experienced in Eugene.

As times changed, the roundup clamped down on fighting. Fines were tripled for disorderly conduct, and more security was brought in. Before I got off patrol, the state police no longer patrolled the roundup, except for entertainment.

//

I was cooking burgers at the high school wrestling booth during the Pendleton Roundup. I looked toward the street and saw a drunk driver come out of Albertson's and continue straight across the street toward a woman sitting on the curb near me. The drunk took a bead on the woman, but a passerby grabbed her dragging her to safety.

The drunken woman veered back into the street at a slow rate of speed. I ran to a gate and caught the woman. I reached into the car and got her to stop; then I took the keys. I had my badge displayed, but I was not in uniform.

It turned out the woman's son was one of the premier cowboys competing at the roundup. I got her out of the car, and she was throwing a fit. I asked someone in the crowd to call the police; apparently they did, but we were drawing quite a crowd. The traffic was so bad it took Pendleton PD about fifteen minutes to arrive.

A crowd started closing in around me, demanding her release. I thought I was about to get mobbed when a big cowboy stepped toward me and turned to the crowd. He told them to back off and that I was just doing my job.

I don't know who he was, but his presence commanded respect. The odds had just turned in my favor. Instead of one crazy cop dressed in a Hawaiian shirt and shorts, now there was a big cowboy who would have been a handful to contend with. The cowboy's actions had made the drunken crowd hesitate long enough for Pendleton PD to arrive.

//

Some guys should not be police officers, and I believe they make it harder for the cops who are out there doing their jobs. In the late 1970s when I was hired, there was some of the mentality that if you could whip the cop, you did not have to take the ticket. I had a truck driver in Eugene who challenged me, so I threw the pinch book (citation book) on his running boards and squared off with him. That was all it took. He knew I was willing to fight him if necessary, so he took the ticket.

There were a couple of troopers who I knew who avoided stopping people as a way to avoid getting cornered for a fight. I was assigned one such individual who was not stopping cars at night, I am not making any judgments. I don't truly know why he wasn't making stops. It was not normal for troopers to ride together, but I was asked to show the individual how I was getting drunks.

We were working a small farming community near Echo. I saw a guy weaving all over the road so I turned around. When the driver saw me he pulled over; I saw him trade places with the passenger. When I got out, I went to the passenger side to contact the DUI suspect who had been driving instead of contacting the person in the driver's seat. My fellow trooper followed me, since we did not work as teams, I shrugged that off.

I told the passenger I wanted to see his driver's license. He refused, saying he was not driving and he would not give it to me. I backed up as he stepped out of the vehicle. His friend from the driver's side got out too and came around behind the trooper. The suspect I was talking to took off his vest and threw it into the back of the pickup. There was no doubt I was going to have to fight this guy.

Behind the trooper the driver's-side suspect had taken off a cowboy belt and wrapped it around his fist with the buckle loose. He had it over his head and was about to hit the other trooper in the back of the head. I elbowed the trooper out of the way and caught the buckle in the palm of my hand. I was able to knock the suspect to the ground and get the belt from him.

I handed the belt to the trooper, who handed it to the DUI suspect, who was now in full rage. He was yelling he was going to take the gun from my partner and shoot me with it. After I took care of the suspect on the ground I turned my attention to the trooper and the suspect. I could not decide who to throw a beating to next.

The trooper quit a couple of weeks later. I have no animosity toward him to this day. Some people should not be police officers.

///

I really liked the officers at the Pendleton Police Department. On slow nights we would go to a local doughnut shop and tell lies. I know—a doughnut shop, how cliché; but it was the only place open all night, and they had good doughnuts.

Sergeant Williams was a legend in the area. He was one of the few officers I knew who, if you got him mad, you would have to kill him to stop him. He grew up as a migrant worker and had worked hard all his life. He was a bit rough around the edges, but he was a great guy.

One night I was eating doughnuts with Pendleton PD, when they got a call of a burglary in progress. Sergeant Williams asked if I would drive him to the burglary call, because he was having car trouble. We took off and found the burglar in the business. While one of his officers took the burglar to jail, he got another burglary call, so off we went. The sun was starting to come up, so I asked Sergeant Williams if he wanted to take his car back to the office to have it worked on. He told me there was nothing wrong with is car, he just wanted someone to talk to.

//

Late one night I was dispatched to a bar fight in Reith. Reith is more of a location than a town or city. Reith had a population of about two hundred people, and at the time it had a bar and a lumber mill. Logic would tell you that when you are dispatched to a bar fight, you should slow down so the guys fighting have time to beat the hell out of each other before you arrive, but I was young so I hustled right over there.

As I got out of my car I could hear yelling from inside the bar. When I walked into the bar there was a guy with his back to me, yelling and facing a small crowd. I walked up directly behind him and stood there while he carried on. He had a beer bottle in his right hand. Apparently to make a point he threw the beer bottle down. I was standing so close to him the bottle hit my boot and rolled across the floor. Even as drunk as he was, he realized he had not gotten the desired effect from throwing the bottle. He slowly turned around my campaign hat was almost touching his face. Those hats were cool when they were not blowing off. When we were looking eye to eye I asked him if he was through; he just hung his head nodded. Sometimes you did not need to be a hard ass, you just needed to appear to be one.

//

One afternoon while working patrol I stopped a car load of Indians who were speeding. As I walked past the trunk I heard a commotion. I contacted the driver and asked him what was in the trunk. He told me a friend of his was drunk, and there was no room for him inside the car, so they put him in the trunk.

I don't think I even wasted my time reprimanding them for their poor judgment. I had the driver unlock the trunk and release his buddy.

I stepped back just in case there were any hard feelings. The driver helped his buddy out of the trunk. There appeared to be no problem; I think he was just happy to breathe fresh air.

You had to see the humor in events like this. You make sure no one is hurt and you get on your way.

CRIMINAL DIVISION

IN 1982 I WAS assigned to the criminal division. I think the station commander was ready to put me under someone else's chain of command. While In the Criminal Division I worked death investigations, thefts, burglaries, sex crimes, narcotics, and prison crimes.

The criminal cases I worked in Pendleton gave me the freedom to move around District IV, while I was following up on cases. I learned better interview techniques by trial and error and watching other detective's interview. It was a great job.

//

My first major case was a child abuse/homicide. We received a call from the Umatilla County Sheriff's Office about a suspect who had brought his dead daughter and a severely wounded daughter to a resident deputy's house.

The deputy and his family lived near Ukiah —a remote location in the county—so he could provide assistance to the citizens in the area in a timely fashion. This suspect knew where the deputy lived, so after he had killed his child and severely wounded the other he brought them to the deputy's house in the early morning hours. It was a traumatic experience for the whole family.

I had seen enough dead people by then, and it was part of the job, but no one wants to see a dead or seriously injured child.

After arriving at the deputy's residence, we were directed to the scene of the crime. It was a gruesome sight. The father of the two little girls had stabbed both of them and thrown them through the window of a cabin into the cold, mountain air. The tiny bloody footprints told a story of a little girl holding and comforting her dying sister. I am not sure how many hours they huddled in the cold that night. As the sun rose the father decided to gather up the girls and take them to the deputy.

Obviously this guy was not wrapped real tight. There were no real answers as to why he did what he did or why he turned himself in. He said the girls were possessed by demons. While executing a search warrant on his residence, we found a Bible that he had highlighted passages about demons.

I don't know how people can work child abuse cases for an extended amount of time, because to be good at interviewing pedophiles and suspects who hurt kids, you need to show them empathy and understanding. You need a confession for a solid case; no one wants to have a child testify.

One of the child abuse detectives I knew in Eugene told me about one of his cases where a baby's head had been slammed through sheetrock, and its lifeless body was hanging on the wall when he arrived. How many cases like that could you do?

I could not tell you how many times we called children's services while making narcotics arrests. It was a common theme. You would find a baby laying in filth and a pacifier would be lying in a window sill next to syringes. Most of these kids don't stand a chance of having a normal life. I don't know how most of them even survive.

//

I was assigned to work cases at the new state prison in Pendleton; this job helped me think outside the box. I was indoctrinated at the state prison in Salem, Oregon. I talked to criminals like the I-5 killer, Randall Woodfield. Talking to Woodfield was like talking to the all-American boy. Looks are deceiving.

One of the first investigations I did in the prison was attempting to find out how drugs were being smuggled in. I went through the list of inmates in an attempt to find out which ones had girlfriends or wives in the local area. I went to their houses and conducted consent searches. I know it is hard to believe but I found drugs in the possession of several of these women. Most of the women had children in the house, so they could have been charged with Endangering the Welfare of a Minor as well as the narcotics charges.

I went back to the prison and contacted the inmates whose wives or girlfriends were in possession of narcotics and informed them that I could charge their wives or girlfriends with a crime, or they could tell me how the drugs were getting into the prison. It was amazing how co-operative inmates were that would not have talked to me a week earlier.

The prison had a woodworking plant, and trucks were coming in to remove sawdust and other materials. Once outside the prison, the trailers were not guarded, so anyone could gain access and hide drugs in the trailers. All they had to do was relay the number of the trailer and the location where the drugs were hidden. With the information I received, I was able to inform the guards at the rear gate, and that avenue was closed. That did not stop drugs from getting into the prison, but it helped for a while.

All this investigation did was fuel my interest in working narcotics. Drugs seemed easy to find; the Oregon State Police had disbanded the narcotics teams five or six years prior to this, so there were no active narcotics teams working in Eastern Oregon.

VEHICLE THEFT UNIT

THIS WAS A START-UP unit that allowed me a lot of creativity. I started out with a few small cases, recovering a car here and a truck there. Then I went to work with Washington State Patrol (WSP) officers in Kennewick. WSP actually has inspection lanes at their office, where they can take a vehicle out of the view of the public and search the vehicle for VIN numbers when people come in for inspections. WSP detectives are experts in locating hidden VIN numbers and working vehicle thefts, after a couple of weeks with their detectives I struck out on my own. I learned to raise ground off VIN numbers, and I used dental casts to copy the hidden VINs for my records.

WSP handed me a case or two where their investigations led to stolen vehicles in Oregon. I was able to seize over $600,000 worth of vehicles in the first year; most of the high-dollar items were heavy equipment. Today that would be a single piece of heavy equipment.

There were vehicles like older Chevrolet pickups for which it was easy to swap VIN numbers off a wreck and change the year ahead, roll the odometer back, and sell for a larger profit. Some of these cases involved organized groups who would steal a vehicle in one area and offload it across the state or into another state.

I found backhoes in mining operations in the Sumpter area. Once you have stolen a piece of heavy equipment and plan to use it on private property, there is no reason for law enforcement or the state to inspect it again.

I had the right to inspect wrecking yards, so I made up wrecking yard inspection sheets with the seal of Oregon in the corner. I used the form to glean more information about the employees; it was very helpful to know who had access to the wrecking yards.

//

My favorite vehicle theft case was a theft ring out of Calgary, Canada. They were stealing motor homes in Canada switching VINs and logos and selling them as different motor homes. I recovered one of these motor homes in Hermiston, Oregon, and was able to trace it back to a suspect in Calgary, Canada. The detective and I were able to gather enough evidence to arrest the suspect in Calgary, which mean I had to go to Calgary to testify.

The Canadian government put me up in a hotel fit for a king. I thought someone broke into my room after dinner when I found the blankets had been turned down and there was a mint on my pillow. I didn't get out much.

Everyone at the Calgary PD was friendly—even the office manager offered to show me the town. The detective gave me the look affirming that would be a bad idea, I graciously decline her offer. The detective told me he would take me on a tour of the grounds of the Calgary Stampede, I made the right choice it was an amazing place.

Drinking seemed to be part of the daily routine. The Calgary police had their own bar and the detectives I was with had beer for lunch. Since I was a guest I figured I should have a drink with them. I did keep looking over my shoulder expecting to see some Oregon State Police Internal Affairs officer hiding in the bushes watching me.

I assume the court was the equivalent to our Federal courts. The Royal Mounted Canadian Police were in full dress uniforms. The Judge wore a white wig like you see in England, and the suspect stood in a small cage in the center of the court room.

After I testified, the judge asked how I was enjoying my stay in Canada. I assured him that everyone had gone out of their way to make my stay memorable. The judge told me to tell my department that I had been ordered by the court to stay a couple more days. I did as I was told.

EXPLOSIVE DISPOSAL

In 1983 I was contacted by Sergeant Zimmerman who was in charge of our bomb squad; he was looking for explosive disposal officers. I got the job, but I don't think there was much competition. My assigned area was District IV, which at the time was most of Eastern Oregon. I got a week-long class on how to dispose of dynamite and blasting caps. I had watched my dad and grandfather blow up stuff as far back as I could remember, so I felt like it was safe.

My first assignment made me rethink the safe part. I was sent to a remote cabin in Summerville. I arrived and found a case of dynamite stuck to the floor. I knew from my week of training that the nitroglycerine leached out and crystallized under the box, so it was probably stuck to the floor boards. I took my secret formula and poured it over the box. I was told that it would hinder an explosive reaction if I moved the box before it evaporated. I used the full two hundred feet of rope on the box to jerk it free. I could hear the box rattling around in the cabin as it came into view of the front door.

I moved the box to a clearing and proceeded to follow the procedure I was taught. As I pulled the sticks apart to lay them out for burning, I could hear the crystals popping. Even I knew this was not a safe move but this was my first assignment, so I followed the procedure and survived the assignment.

I went back into the cabin and saw that the box had been resting on a blasting cap, which had been dragged eight feet across the room. That was the first of hundreds of calls to old mines, cabins, farm houses, and other improvised explosive disposal calls I was dispatched to.

//

I liked to work the old mining claims. Most of them were in the area around Baker City. A lot of miners had figured ways to live there year-round. Some were generating electricity with streams that ran through their claims. One such claim ran a four-inch pipe upstream that tapered down to a half-inch about two hundred feet downstream. The pipe went into a small building near the creek that held batteries and a car generator. The water was spinning a wheel that was attached to the generator. They had all the comforts of home.

The owner of the mine took me into his mine and showed me twenty-one cases of dynamite that had been stacked in three piles, seven high. The nitro had leached, and all the boxes were stuck together. I got out three hundred feet of rope, which got me just outside the mine. I poured the approved chemical formula over the pile and gave a jerk on the rope it felt like I had tied it to a bulldozer.

I told the mine owner the only option was to burn it in place. I did tell him there was a chance that if enough heat built up it could detonate. I poured diesel over the stack and lit it from a remote location. Normally a dynamite fire burns fast, this lasted long enough that we had lunch while smoke poured from the mine.

Did you notice the difference from the first dynamite call to the Baker City call? I had not yet been allowed to go to bomb school, but I had already decided I would not pull crystallized or sweaty dynamite apart again.

On some of the mine calls I had to crawl into shafts where the dynamite was stored. The fumes from the nitroglycerine would cause an instant headache. It was part of the job I did not enjoy. Mine shafts were dangerous. One mine was so dark that it even swallowed up my light. As I walked down the shaft, I almost stepped into a vertical shaft. I stepped back and flashed my light into the hole. I could not see the bottom.

//

One of the perks of working in District IV was that it was so large that I would get transported to EOD (Explosive Ordinance Disposal) calls by airplane. As an example of a typical long-distance disposal, our pilot flew me to southern Oregon. We landed on the road, and a rancher picked us up. I did my thing, and we flew home for dinner. If I would have had to drive to this call, it would have taken two days. Access to aircraft was a huge asset.

We never had a pilot on the state police that I did not completely trust. I actually enjoyed the change of pace and the company.

//

Part of my job as an explosive disposal officer was to travel the state, putting on booby trap classes for state, county, and federal officers. Some of the forest service big wigs came from Washington, DC. for one of our classes. We used live explosives, fish hooks in the brush, noise makers (cans filled with rocks), snakes (yes, real snakes) tied to the brush, remote detonation, trip wires, and pits filled with boards and nails. We would flag the dangerous area and send a guide with each group. These exercises were designed to show officers what they could encounter when entering Marijuana grows. All of our scenarios were taken from actual Marijuana grow.

I enjoyed putting on the booby trap classes not only was I putting my skills to the test, I got to meet a lot of troopers, deputies and officers who I would have not otherwise met.

//

In the 1990s Elden Alexander was assigned as my new bomb-squad partner. Elden was not new to me; he was just new to the bomb squad. Elden and I were like brothers. We also worked narcotics together on the task force. We had lots of long drives around Eastern Oregon, where we cured the ills of this world. It's amazing how messed up everyone else was.

We did not get much civil war ordnance, but when we did they were extremely dangerous to handle; the old black powder never went bad. A chief of police called who was in possession of a cannon ball. Based on his description, we called the FBI's Hazardous Device School. They were a great reference as they dealt with civil war munitions all the time.

The technician we called knew exactly what we were dealing with, right down to the rattling noise it made if it was shaken. Elden and I told the chief to put it in a safe place, because it was extremely dangerous. We arrived in less than an hour. When we walked into his office, he was on the phone and had the cannonball in the other hand shaking it. Apparently it was not his time to go.

//

One evening Elden and I received a call from a high school in Umatilla, Oregon, that asked us to pick up some picric acid, and in passing the caller mentioned several other chemicals. At the time it was not unusual for us to destroy chemicals for high schools. Some of the chemicals were over forty years old and were quite flammable and explosive.

The next morning on the way to Umatilla we called a chemical company about one the chemicals they had mentioned. The chemical was so dangerous they did not make it anymore. We talked to our contact person and found out there were several unknown chemicals, and they had been knocked over and mixed into an unknown concoction. This was sounding more and more like something we wanted nothing to do with. The chemistry lab was being torn down to make way for new construction. A crane had bumped the corner of the room and the chemicals went everywhere.

By the time we arrived around 8:30 a.m. we had decided the only thing we were willing to do was burn them in place. We called the local hazardous materials (hazmat) team, which was comprised of firefighters from Hermiston. They arrived, suited up, and went inside to film the chemical spill.

Elden and I stood our ground. The only thing we were willing to do was burn them in place. We got calls from hazmat companies who specialized in the removal of chemicals, our supervisors in Salem, the school board, and insurance companies. The school district could not

51

find a hazmat team in the country who would remove unknown chemicals that had mixed together.

By 3:00 p.m. the local hazmat team and Umatilla PD started evacuating residents from the area. The principle told us we had permission from the school board to burn the chemicals in place. Elden and I borrowed full hazmat gear from the fire department and went into the chemistry room. We set up cans of gasoline wrapped in detonating cord and waited for the all clear. The local fire department charged their fire hoses, and we detonated the charge. I have to say that was an amazing explosion and fire ball. The roof lifted off the building.

There was no other recourse. It's not worth risking the lives of police or firefighters to save some property.

//

The bomb squad grew over the years; the training got better and the equipment improved. I repeatedly requested to attend the FBI's Hazardous Device School. My requests fell on deaf ears, until I was involved in a tragic incident involving our bomb-squad supervisor, Dick Schuening.

On October 2, 1997, we received a call from a federal agency asking for assistance. They had an inmate in federal custody, who was willing to show them where he had buried a cache of explosives in the remote mountains west of Sumpter Oregon. This seemed like every other explosive disposal call we went on. With the suspect's help, Dick and I located and dug up the old blasting caps. Dick said he would prepare a site to countercharge the caps. The forest was very dry and would likely burn if we detonated them where they were.

I removed the caps from the hole and walked them about 150 yards to a creek bottom where Dick had prepared a hole to counter-charge the blasting caps. As Dick was preparing the counter-charge he told me to tell the rest of the crew that we would be done in a few minutes. As I arrived back at the staging area we hear an explosion.

I had not heard Dick give the fire-in-the-hole warning, so I started in that direction with one of the federal officers. When we arrived, we found Dick mortally injured; he had absorbed most of the blast. The young agent attended to some of Dick's wounds, while I held him until he passed. Dick lived long enough to relay his love for his family.

We knew that old blasting caps are extremely dangerous and can detonate when introduced to static electricity or movement. Shortly after Sergeant Scheuning was killed, I received a call from a bomb squad back east that had a similar experience with blasting caps. The officer who called said he was outside the blast area and three other officers were near the blasting caps when they detonated due to static electricity or movement. All three were on fire when he turned around. One of the officers was blinded all three were seriously injured.

//

Due to accidents like this the explosive disposal officers on the Oregon State Police were sent to the FBI's Hazardous Device School. We got updated equipment and training on a regular, scheduled basis.

I never let it creep into my head that anything was going to happen to me. You could call it denial, but I think it is more of a self-defense mechanism. This way you are not second guessing your own decisions. You see referees in football and baseball that make decisions in a split second, and they normally get it right. A police officer makes life and death decisions in a split second. They also don't have time for second guesses . Every police officer I know that is good at what he does, is good at thinking on his feet.

Shortly after Dick's death, Elden and I were on an explosive disposal call in Troy, Oregon. We found hundreds of pounds of old, decaying dynamite to dispose of. I asked the owner if there were any blasting caps, and he was not sure. I saw a gunny sack hanging in the rafters. I had seen blasting caps stored in gunny sacks before so I grabbed the sack and cut the rope it almost pulled me off the stool I was standing on. The sack weighed about 25 pounds and it was full of blasting caps.

I took them out and dug a hole for disposal and placed the caps in the bottom. Elden made up a countercharge to place on the caps. I made up a sack of sand to help push the explosion down. I placed the explosives on the gunny sack and gently set the bag of sand on top of the explosives. As I released the bag the whole pile shifted.

I don't think I had ever experienced real fear in my life until that moment. In a split second I was completely drenched in sweat. It happened so fast I didn't have time to react. I just knelt there and reflected on what had happened to Dick. I should never have put myself in that situation knowing what I had learned about blasting caps. Elden and I changed our procedures after that call and found new methods and tools to remotely set up our counter-charges.

//

I could not tell you how many suspicious packages we opened over the years, and it doubled over night after 9-11. Elden and I were actually called to the airport the day of 9-11, after the World Trade center had been destroyed, and the Pentagon was damaged.

A young man from the Middle East sent a suitcase ahead of him to the Pendleton airport. After opening the abandoned suitcase we found photos of the World Trade Center and Middle-Eastern men with tourist destinations in New York in the background. There were several video tapes in the suitcase as well. We turned the information over to the FBI and were later told that the suitcase belonged to a college student. That may have been true, but 9-11 changed the way we reacted to situations that may have been considered routine in the past.

//

Another narcotics partner turned part-time bomb tech was Mike Schultz. Mike and I had been training with a new, shock-tube initiator. This device is used to ignite shock tube that in turn detonates a blasting cap. The shock tube was safer than using electric blasting caps to detonate a charge. Mike had used the shock-tube initiator for a couple of training scenarios and was very familiar with it.

That evening we got a call about an Improvised Explosive Device (IED) in a small community near Ontario, Oregon. Since Mike had not yet been to the FBI's Hazardous Device School, he could not assist me on a call. So I called a bomb tech out of the valley, and he flew over. It was decided that we should countercharge the device. I put on the bomb suit and took the countercharge down to the IED, leaving the detonator with Mike. I knew I could trust Mike with my life. We had worked together for years, and he had trained with the shock tube initiator.

While I was taking the countercharge to the device, the bomb tech reached for the shock tube initiator that Mike was holding. Mike told the bomb tech he had been training with it and would keep the initiator. The bomb tech insisted and took the shock tube initiator from Mike.

I had just set the countercharge and had walked back about thirty yards from the device when it detonated. I saw a blank expression on the bomb tech's face as he looked at the shock tube initiator. He did not know how to use the initiator and had removed the safety, initiating the explosion. I should have kicked his ass; since he had never used that particular initiator, he should have never touched it. At that point nothing needed to be said; he understood what he had done.

Over the years Elden and I had learned whom to work with and whom to avoid on the bomb squad. Some people just took more chances than others. Elden and I helped write the new EOD policy for the state police after the death of Dick Scheuning. We followed the new policy to the letter, and the new technicians in District IV followed it to the letter too.

When I retired we had one full time bomb tech and two part-time technicians to work Eastern Oregon. With terrorist threats and domestic anarchists, it is a full-time job. The equipment you need to maintain is extensive. The bomb truck always needed work; robots need maintenance; batteries in all the equipment need charging; equipment for calls needed to be replaced; x-ray machines needed maintenance; and someone needed to stay on top of the new technology. Every bomb tech is required to have a minimum of sixteen hours of training monthly. Bomb techs also gave public talks and did robot demos for the high school robotics class.

I continued on the bomb squad until I retired in 2004. In addition to these duties, the Oregon State Police Special Weapons and Tactics team sent me to Explosive Entry School at Gunsite Academy Arizona. I was assigned as an explosive breacher.

NARCOTICS IN THE BEGINNING

In 1985 I was contacted by the District IV criminal sergeant about whether I was willing to be part of a new Oregon State Police narcotics unit. I couldn't say yes fast enough.

Now I'm going to get on a soapbox for a minute and talk about legalizing narcotics. Why not legalize marijuana? Actually marijuana is not the same stuff I and many others grew up with. This stuff is ten times as potent as it was in the sixties and seventies. Every addict I met whether they were hooked on cocaine, methamphetamine, or heroin told me they started out on marijuana, hence the gate way drug argument.

Marijuana significantly impairs your motor skills and a recent study shows people are impaired up to twenty-four hours after smoking Marijuana. If it is legal to smoke, your surgeon, a pilot, a truck driver, the police, or your baby sitter could be using it. Where do you draw the line?

As it turned out I knew nothing about street-level narcotics. I have never smoked a joint, and I did not know any slang terms. In other words, I had a big learning curve.

We had very little money and no informants. A local FBI agent Mike McPheters, who wrote the book *Agent Bishop*, hooked me up with an informant who was recently released from federal prison for committing armed robberies. Agent McPheters thought Bobby could point me in the right direction.

Bobby turned out to be my first Narcotics partner. I know anyone who knows anything about narcotic would consider this a receipt for disaster, and it should have been. But this was decades ago, and we were breaking new ground.

On my first narcotics purchase, Bobby took me to Hermiston to buy a quarter gram of crank (methamphetamine). I was hearing sayings like, "This stuff has legs," which meant it would keep you going. Little of what I heard made sense. They were talking about getting a better deal on an eight-balls (eighth of an ounce) of crank. I didn't know what was going on. The suspect handed Bobby a paper fold. A paper fold was a very common way to package powdered narcotics. I handed the suspect twenty dollars then took the paper fold from Bobby and put it in my pocket. Everyone involved looked at me a little funny, but nothing was said until Bobby and I got back into the van. Bobby asked if I was trying to get us killed. He said you never buy anything without checking it out first.

Since I had no formal training, Bobby was my narcotics coach. Without him I would have either failed or been killed. We spent a lot of nights working in bars. I learned how to approach people cold and get them to sell me drugs. I had a million lines for different scenarios. I learned I had to be very careful how I hid my weapon. Women in the bar would come up and put their hands all over you, not because they thought you were hot, but because they were looking for a wire or a gun.

To save me time hanging out in bars all night I would send Bobby into a new town a day ahead of me. By the time I got there he would have befriended half the town. Bobby was a conman, and he was good at it. With Bobby's help I learned quickly how to stay out of trouble. Staying out of trouble was important since I had no back up; there were no radios and no cell phones. I kept a roll of quarters in my car so I could use pay phones. Good luck finding a pay phone today.

Working with Bobby was a blessing and a curse. I would never again work with an informant in whom I put the kind of trust I did with Bobby. I had informants who bought a lot more narcotics, but I never trusted any of them. Over the next few years we started doing less undercover work and began using more informants to make our cases. We started having two officers present at all times. We could monitor their every move, which meant strip searching informants coming and going, so no drugs or money was ever unaccounted for.

It was a lot easier in the beginning, because I could go into a town and make buys myself. By "easier," I mean it was easier for court. Early in my career it was fine because my wife and kids were home, so I could work the bars and get home by 3 a.m., get some sleep, see the wife and kids, and then hit it again.

Being a dirt bag and not washing my clothes was tough. My wife was a saint, but she also knows I don't like nasty women. When I would tell her I had to meet some skanky woman in LaGrande that evening, it might give my wife some piece of mind, but then again it might not. How many wives would put up with that shit? Normally I did not say a thing about what I was doing, but that actually bothered her more.

As time went on I felt sorry for my kids. They would invite me to school to have lunch, and the other parents would clutch their kids when I walked into the room. I guess kids don't know any different. You are still their dad, no matter what you look like.

My wife and I were having dinner one night in Pendleton and a friend of ours walked up then looked at me and walked away. Later she told Shari that she thought she was cheating on me, because she did not recognize me.

I preyed on women's insecurity. I could go into a bar for an hour or two, watch the crowd, and pick out the women who would vouch for me. Most of these gals had never had anyone treat them like a person, let alone be nice to them. I could buy them a beer and play a game of pool or shuffle board with them, and then we were friends. I was probably the first guy that they ever met that was not trying to get into their pants. I cannot tell you how many women I had tell local drug dealers that I was their cousin or an old friend so I could buy drugs from them.

I knew women in Pendleton that would not have given me the time of day when I was in uniform. After I started working narcotics and looked like hell I had a gal from church hit on me. My wife found out about that one because I mentioned it to a buddy of mine in the office who told his wife. Do women like the thought of being with someone who may be a little dangerous, or do they secretly like dirt bags? I can't answer the question; I'm just throwing it out there.

Even though my wife was pissed at the church lady, I think I got some credit for not taking her up on her offer—she *was* very attractive.

Scorned women also made my job easier. We worked with several of them, and if a gal found out that her man had cheated on her or had done her wrong, she would turn on them in a heartbeat. These women were a little tricky to use. You had to use them quickly, because most of them were hooked on coke or methamphetamine, and they would do almost anything to keep a supply. But vengeance was overwhelming for them. Every person you used, either men or woman, had a motive for helping, and it was extremely important that you knew what that motive was. Some did it for the money, while others did it to eliminate competition; whatever the reason you needed to know why.

The biggest reason I used so many women to help me infiltrate narcotics operations was because they could be so charming even when they knew they were lying to these guys. Don't get the impression, however, that I had no empathy for these women.

There was one young lady I arrested for possession of methamphetamine who was very attractive the first time we contacted her. Within a year's time we had arrested her three times. I put her pictures side by side. The change was staggering. At the end of the year she had aged at least ten years, lost most of her teeth, and had scars all over her body from picking at it.

Methamphetamine makes you feel like there is something under your skin. It is very common to see these people with scabs all over their faces and arms. One guy took it to an extreme. A fellow officer was called by a suspect, because he was afraid. Even though he had called the police the suspect would not open the door. By the time the officer got into the house the suspect had taken a knife to his own leg, opened it up, and was using salad tongs to pull out muscle; he was looking for what was under his skin.

I remember cleaning up methamphetamine labs with my bare hands and with no mask. I recovered one lab and went to the office to store

my evidence. The lieutenant and troops were running out of the office with burning eyes. They could not breathe. I was desensitized since I had been handling it all day. A few years later at a narcotics conference, we learned that the whole California methamphetamine unit had died from various cancers and liver diseases. Their supervisor gave the class; he had not been exposed to the same amount of chemicals as his team.

I had been working narcotics for years by now. By this time things changed. Everyone had to have special training and wear full protective suits with respirators and only samples were taken. Hazmat companies were called to dispose of the rest of the chemicals. As far as I know my liver is still working properly. I was stuck with needles several times during searches. I was lucky I never ended up with AIDS or hepatitis. I even had to leave my boots outside my house and wash my own work clothes, so my family would not be exposed to these dangers. These are not things I thought about when I started working narcotics.

I have to relate a couple of quick stories relating to biological hazards, while I'm thinking about it. For one of the first search warrants, I did not have a team, so I recruited troopers who worked in the same area to assist me. I think they enjoyed it because it was a change of pace.

While I acquired the evidence, I would have them search. On one occasion I heard laughter coming from the master bedroom. Curiosity got the best of me, so I went to see what they had discovered. I saw two troopers squared off, fencing with two of the largest dildos I had ever seen. I took a few moments to chuckle and then ask them where they thought the weapons had been. They stopped, looked at their swords, and dropped them; neither one of them was wearing gloves.

While at the scene of the search warrant, an informant contacted me and told me the suspect in this case was heading to Ontario, Oregon with a load of methamphetamine. I gave one of the troopers a description of the vehicle and asked him to get on the freeway to see if he could intercept her. About a half hour later around 10 a.m., I received a call that he had located and stopped our suspect.

I met the trooper and our suspect on the freeway and conducted a search of the vehicle. I then turned my attention to the suspect. This gal had huge breasts. I made sure the trooper was close, so he could witness the search of the woman.

I asked her to turn around, undo her bra, untuck her shirt, and lean forward. I had seen a lot of woman use their bras to transport drugs and money. Instead of doing what I asked she turned toward the Trooper and lifted her shirt and bra up and over her head.

You would have thought the trooper had seen a gun. He stepped back about five feet into the freeway. Since it was daylight everyone driving buy on the freeway saw her breasts too. I'm sure the trooper thought he was going to be fired. She got the desired reaction from the trooper. She smiled looked at me and said, "Is that good enough, Mike?" I had to say it was. I don't think the trooper appreciated that I asked him to transport her to jail for the drugs we found at her house.

//

The story above reminded me of another biohazard. I had information of a young woman who was dealing methamphetamine. I did not want to burn my informant by writing a search warrant, so I asked a detective to go with me to see if we could gain consent to search her apartment.

We contacted the young woman and obtained consent to search. During the search we found scales, packaging, and methamphetamine residue. From the information I had received I was convinced there was more methamphetamine there. She had taken a long time to open the door after we had identified ourselves, so I knew she could have hidden it anywhere. I had seen lots of hiding places, so we had checked most of the common ones.

I notices she was wearing a night shirt so I knew she did not hide the Methamphetamine in her bra, she was not wearing one. Somehow I convinced her that I knew she had hidden the methamphetamine while we were at the door. Without warning she put her foot on the bed and reached up between her legs and pulled out a baggie of methamphetamine. I had not realized she was not wearing any panties until that moment. She held out the baggie for us to take. I looked at the other detective, who put his hands in his pockets. I asked her to place it on the dresser, while we got some gloves and an evidence bag. I had seen a lot, but that took me by surprise.

WORKING UNDERCOVER

Working undercover started out by choosing another identity. I picked an identity that I was familiar with. My fake ID had my first name as a middle name in case someone I knew ran into me, which happened on several occasions. This is a small world we live in. The place I chose to be from had to be familiar to me, because people quizzed me about it often, so I chose my old address in Eugene.

As far as my cover story went, it was very easy. I either posed as a repo man who sold cars back for a living or as a construction worker. If a community had a freeway project of a large construction company working in the area, it made sense to see a few new faces in the bars.

To emphasize the use of an undercover name, I was working alone in a bar in Enterprise, Oregon, where the population is probably a thousand people with lots of tourists. A farmer from Pendleton came into the bar and called me by my first name. I had to do a little explaining that some of my buddies called me by my middle name. On more than one occasion I was told to take the money out of my wallet and hand it to them; these are paranoid people. I kept old tickets with my undercover identity on them and business cards from Eugene.

My buddy realized at once that I was working a narcotics operation after a few introductions he challenged the suspects to a game of pool. My buddy had plenty of money, and I could not use state funds to gamble with unless gamblers were the target. He dropped a couple of hundred dollars on the suspects, and I lost one of my favorite tee shirts. I could not put my friend in danger and never approached the suspects about narcotics at that time, but down the road they trusted me, and I was able to make a case.

//

I wrote my first narcotics warrant and went to Judge Olsen's house to get it signed. As I sat there with him reading the warrant, I fell like a kid in school having a paper graded. After he read the warrant he looked at me and said, "Can you swear to me that there are drugs in this house right now?" I had to tell him no. Judge Olsen said, "Come back when you can."

I was embarrassed that I did not understand the requirements for a search warrant. I vowed to never have that happen again, and it never

did. I plagiarized every narcotics search warrant I could get my hands on. We became very good at writing search warrants. Some of our warrants on major suspects could be over a hundred pages. It seemed like the majority of them were taken to the judges' homes in the middle of the night, but I never heard a complaint.

//

I worked undercover for the Union Pacific Rail Road police. The rail road investigators were great guys. They were headquartered out of St. Louis. Gary, the contact officer, had worked narcotics for years in the St. Louis area and had worked a very rough area. When you think of private police, you don't give them much credit for knowing what they are doing, but Gary was a different story.

With the help of the UPRR we were able to make several cases against employees. I had an easy time working in LaGrande. I told a couple of the old timers that I was the great grandson of Tom Harrison. The Harrisons were well known for poaching and running whiskey. One of my great uncles was involved in a gunfight over a woman on the main street of LaGrande, so I fit right in.

The UPRR had a lot of employees in LaGrande, Oregon, and wanted to infiltrate them. I was given UPRR road ID from St. Louis, traffic tickets and pocket trash like I had done for my Eugene ID, and I went to work. As luck would have it I ran into a guy from the St. Louis area. I had to dance around the topic and be vague with the guy. After that I stuck with my old ID for every operation.

We made several methamphetamine buys that lead us back to some violent railroad personnel who lived in Pendleton. It was a very successful operation for us and the UPRR. I don't know if we would have ever made the arrests we made without the UPRR angle. The UPRR personnel were a very tight community.

//

I think my favorite prop or cover story was our "rubber-duck" operation. The state police sent two troopers to truck-driving school. They leased a truck and trailer, and then we started working truck stops around the state and into Idaho. I posed as the co-driver. I would help drop the trailer and act as the gopher. I did the buys but used Bob, our driver, as my witnesses.

The first truck stop we came to was in the Hermiston area. I talked to the attendant and asked if I could score some crank to help us get down the road. He said no problem and asked if we wanted a diesel deal too. I had to ask him what he meant. He said that if he ran the pump slow it would not run the meter and the diesel would be free, and we could pay him for his trouble. He sent us into the café to have some pie, because it would take a while. When we came out we had a tank full of diesel and crank. I paid him for the crank and gave him twenty dollars for the diesel and down the road we went. We later charged him for embezzlement and delivery of methamphetamine. Who knows how much he had cost the company.

I hate to be too hard on a trooper thrust into the middle of a narcotics operation, but one of the drivers started to freak out on us when we were in a bar in Baker, Oregon. Bill and I had hooked up with some guys who had to take us to their house to score the dope we had requested, so I told the other driver to sit there and have a beer until we came back.

I had told the suspects that Bill was a lightweight and wanted some pot and that I needed some crank. So away we went; the deal went smooth—especially after they realized I was from Eugene. As it turned out I had been involved in a case were their brother had been arrested, and I knew background information about mutual friends.

When we got back to the bar, the other driver looked like a cat stuck to the ceiling. He was telling me how people were looking at him, but no one had approached him or talked to him. That was the last time I worked with the fellow. Some guys are not cut out to lie and deceive people, and I guess he was one of them.

We moved our rubber duck operation down the road to work truck stops in Ontario, Oregon. Ontario is just east of Idaho. I met a fellow right away who was eager to get Bob and me some crank, but he had to take us across the border into Idaho. No problem. We had a chase car with some surveillance equipment following us, so away we went. Bob sat up front with the suspect. Getting into a vehicle with some unknown doper was never a good idea.

We headed east into Idaho. At first we were leisurely driving to his dealer's house, but the farther we went the faster our suspect was driving. I looked over his shoulder and saw we were going over a hundred miles per hour. I knew the surveillance car could not keep up. I'm a control freak and did not like having a doper hauling ass over hill and dale.

I pulled a knife on our suspect and placed it on his throat. I told him in no uncertain terms that he had better slow down because the cops were going to stop us, and I had a warrant out of my arrest. I made him pull over while I chewed his ass. We had just crested a hill when he pulled over. Sure enough, in less than a minute came the surveillance car airborne over the hill at over one hundred miles per hour. I apparently had the full attention of our suspect, because he never noticed a thing. We made the transaction and headed back with our suspect apologizing all the way.

We then took the truck to Klamath Falls. I was not familiar with the area, so we met with local detectives who could identify suspects as we approached them.

We made one case at a truck stop, and then went to town to hit a local bar. It did not take long to make contact with a kid who said he could score us some coke. During our conversation we learned that he was from LA and was in Klamath Falls to play football at the college.

We went to a vehicle we used as a surveillance vehicle and loaded up. He asked me for my wallet, I took the money out and handed it to him. He checked my ID to see if it matched my story. He was a little nervous since we had just met. He directed us to a residential area and went into a house. He came out a short while later and told us to drive back toward the bar where we had met.

We pulled into a parking lot where he handed me the coke, and I gave him the money. We had talked to the local detectives while the suspect was in the house and decided we needed to arrest him after the exchange, because they did not know him.

As our suspect got out of the vehicle the local detectives approached him and ordered him to the ground. The chase was on. The kid started running with me and another detective on his heels. That kid could run, but I had good endurance. After several blocks he realized he could not lose us, so he dove into an alley and hid in some boxes. I saw him make the turn so it didn't take me too long to find him. The other detective arrived to assist with the arrest. I had no idea where I was, but neither did the kid. He had run to the back of the police department. The detective just walked him into the back door.

//

Due to the geographic location of Pendleton, we would end up in Idaho and Washington State at times. The Sheriff from Oregon cross-deputized the Washington detectives, and Sheriff Jackson from Washington deputized me and a couple other detectives.

One night another detective and I were working bars in Milton-Freewater. We struck a deal with two guys, Jose and Hector, to purchase crank. They told us to follow them to College Place, Washington, which was about five miles away. There was nothing out of the ordinary about this arrangement.

We ended up in an area of College Place. I was not familiar with but it appeared to be a dead-end street. They wanted to take the cash and then return with the drugs. We did not like to let the money walk, so we told them no. We did not know who Jose and Hector were. They took us by a house with the door open and the light on, and said they would be going there. After some more negations we agreed to the arrangement.

You can guess what happened next: there was a back way out of the area. Jose and Hector went down the street, drove past the house, and gunned it, leaving us with nothing. The next day we found out that Jose and Hector worked at a mill in Walla Walla. My partner and I were waiting for them in the parking lot at the end of their shift. As they approached their car they saw us, thinking we were drug dealers coming to kick their asses. They took off their coats and prepared for an ass whipping. We identified ourselves as police officers and displayed our badges and had to kick their asses anyway. The scene turned ugly quick, and the crowd of workers closed in on us as we subdued our suspects.

We drew our weapons and badges and told the crowd to back off. In the distance I could hear sirens heading our way. Apparently someone had called the cops about the two guys in the parking lot with guns. I was happy to see a couple of familiar faces. I went back to Sheriff Jackson and asked if we were still welcome in his county. He just shook his head shot us a smile and walked away.

//

71

I was asked to work on a case with some of my narcotics friends in Washington. I was told that one of their local dealers and his girl-friend, Vickie, had a domestic dispute of some kind, and she came to the narcotics officers and told them she would help set up a buy. The lead detective told me that they had been trying to get a buy from the suspect, Juan, for a couple of years.

Juan had insulated himself from the regular dealers, and they had not been able to get a buy. Juan was a scratch golfer and appeared to be a somewhat legitimate business man to the general public.

Vickie had agreed to introduce me to Juan as her cousin from "back east." I would stay at Vickie's house and the rest was up to me. My golf game was very weak, so we spent a day golfing to prep me for an outing with Juan.

I met Vickie and all went well. We got our stories together, and I moved into a spare bedroom. Later that day Vickie called Juan and asked if he would be willing to take her cousin golfing. Juan agreed, and we spent the afternoon together on the golf course. After our game I asked Juan if he could hook me up with come coke as I wanted to hit the bars that evening and wanted to entertain the ladies. Juan hooked me up with some cocaine within an hour.

I called the Walla Walla narcotics detectives and told them I had made the buy. The detectives seemed excited. But they wanted another buy, in Washington a second delivery doubled the sentencing.

I told them I would try I told Juan I was going to hit the town another night and was looking to score more coke. He again agreed and said he would get the coke and he would go out with Vickie and me. That was not what I was hoping for but I agreed. Juan picked us up, and we went to Kennewick, Washington for the evening. As the night progressed Juan mentioned getting some of the coke back. I told him I had used it and had nothing to share.

After we returned to Vickie's house Juan spent the night with her. I felt a little uneasy about Juan at that point. I put my gun under the pillow and went to sleep. Sometime around four in the morning I was awaken by a cat jumping on my face. I may have killed that cat as it hit the far wall, I don't recall. I had a bad feeling about my situation. Juan was hooked up with some very dangerous people. At about 5:30 a.m. I decided I would leave a note for Vickie letting her know I was going to work out.

When Juan woke up and realized I was gone he went crazy and stormed out of the house looking for me. Vickie called the detectives and told them what had happened. While I was working out at a local gym, a couple of police cars with uniformed officers and the detectives showed up and told me Juan was looking for me.

I turned over the evidence and left the area. I later learned that Juan had left his family and moved back to Mexico to avoid arrest.

//

Over the years I was hired a couple of times to kill people. One of those was a case in Walla Walla, Washington. I was contacted by the Walla Walla sheriff's office and asked if I would be willing to pose as a hit man.

The sheriff's office had already done the background work. They knew who Martin was, where he was, and who he wanted killed. Apparently the suspect lived out of state and had approached a biker and told him he was looking to hire someone to kill a guy named Paul in Walla Walla. The biker told the police, and they contacted Walla Walla County Sheriff's Office. From their background investigation they learned that the Paul was living with Martin's ex-girlfriend.

The introduction was set up by phone, and I was recommended by the biker. The only thing Martin told me was that he wanted Paul killed.

He gave me and address and a physical description. I took a day to do the surveillance and called Martin back. I told him it would not be a problem, but from what I had seen but it would be easier to kill them both. Wow did that draw a response. Martin did not want the girl hurt; he begged me not to kill her.

We settled on a price and a place to meet to set this in motion. Martin was flying into the area in a couple of days. The next day he said he could not make the face-to-face meeting, but he would wire me most of the money up front, and after Paul was killed he would send me the rest. I made it very clear that when I received the money there was no turning back. He said he understood and sent the check. I never got to meet Martin. The authorities on the other end apprehended him. Martin was transported to Walla Walla and pleaded guilty.

//

I was working undercover during the Pendleton Roundup. I went to the local Indian bar, and as I worked my way through the crowd, I got near the back of the bar and realized I was the only white guy in there. I had long hair and a beard but it was reddish blond not black. I said hi to a couple of Indians in a booth near the stool where I had sat.

One of them looked over at me stared for a minute than said "Custer what are you doing in here?" I told him I came in to buy him a beer. I bought him a beer sat down and drank one with him then left the bar. The last confrontation Custer had with the Indians did not work out so well for Custer. I saved my hair and the tax payers bought him another beer.

//

I was working in an area with another detective when we contacted a woman who told us she could hook us up with some methamphetamine. She had us follow her to her house. When we arrived it was becoming clear she either did not have any methamphetamine, or she was not going to get us any. She had us grab a beer, then went down a hallway, and returned with a handgun.

I have no idea what was going through her head. As she walked past me she pointed the handgun at my partner. I grabbed the gun and wrestled it from her, she was screaming at that top of her lungs that it was her gun and she wanted it back. I unloaded the gun and took the ammo. As we were leaving I gave her back her gun.

We later ran a check on her. She had no record of any contact with the police. I never went back, and I still have no idea what was going through her mind. Maybe my partner had insulted her. I'm kidding, of course, but we will never know.

Working undercover is not hard science. If you misread a person or a situation, you are gambling with your life. We dealt with a lot more dangerous people than this woman, but on this night at this time she was extremely dangerous, because we had misjudged her.

//

Not all my undercover cases involved narcotics. Since I was the explosives guy too, I was interested when I heard a guy in Pilot Rock would build a pipe bomb for anyone who asked. Our informant made an introduction to the suspect. I made it very clear I was looking for a device to kill a guy who ripped me off in a drug deal. The suspect made it clear he had no problem with his part in a homicide.

The suspect and I sat down so he could show me the design of this device and we struck a deal on the price. He told me he would be done in a couple of days. I called our bomb techs out of Salem who came to take the device after I made the deal. The suspect called in a couple of days, and I bought the device. The suspect was arrested without incident.

BLUE MOUNTAIN ENFORCEMENT NARCOTICS TEAM

IN 1985 ALL THE local agencies in Umatilla County realized there was enough narcotics work to require a task force. Narcotics activity generated burglaries, thefts, robberies, domestic disputes, assaults and homicides. The task force started by partnering with Pendleton PD, then the Umatilla County Sheriff's Office and as it grew Milton-Freewater PD, Hermiston PD, Morrow County Sheriff's Office and Umatilla PD came on board. The Blue Mountain Enforcement Narcotics Team (BENT) was born.

The task force proved to be a valuable resource not just for monitoring narcotics operations but also as a source for valuable information about other crimes in our community. It was a very good partnership; by providing a detective to the task force the departments gained six more detectives. If a community was having a specific problem in their area, we would come in and target the problem. Most of the departments did not have the manpower or resources to work narcotics on their own.

In the beginning we still did our own buys or accompanied informants on buys. As the task force grew, we realized how much danger we were putting ourselves in and started using either paid informants who worked for a salary or informants who were working off charges.

Our first informant who worked for a salary was able to make buys from over fifty people in the Umatilla County. We were going hard for a few months. We would make drug buys all night and catch up on paper work until that evening and start all over again.

We wanted to let the community know we were making a difference, so we decided to round up all the suspects in one day. We knew it would be good press but a burden on the DA's office and the jail. We made up packets that contained suspect photos and charges, and we sent out teams of officers to arrest the suspects. It was a great success.

Now it was time to find out if we were doing our jobs. I think every defense attorney in Umatilla County had a shot at us. It was imperative that we showed them we were above board and professional. If we started losing cases we would have to go to court on every suspect we ever arrested. It seemed like we were in court for about nine months. All the suspects were either convicted or pleaded guilty.

There was a big learning curve for all the officers as they rotated into the unit. Most departments did not want to leave their officers in the task force too long. It took two years for rotating officers to see everything and work well with the group in tactical situations.

It was nice having young guys rotate into the unit. It made me stay current on case law, tactical procedures, and new technology. By now we had pagers and a few bag phones hard wired into our cars, so we could communicate with each other.

Informants were a necessary evil. They were hard to manage; two officers were required every time we met with them, and we always had to remember they were criminals. One of the conferences we went to really brought home how important it is to follow procedures with informants. Most informants knew we had money to buy drugs. Sometimes we would have thirty thousand dollars or more with us.

A detective back east had worked with an informant for over ten years. One night the detective decided to meet with the informant alone. The informant had gotten himself in a situation where he needed cash. When the detective came alone, the informant shot and robbed him.

We tried to treat informants with respect, due to that fact we would have informants show up after ten years and want to work again. Informants always knew we were in charge, and we would check out their stories. Before an informant was used, we completed a packet on them and got approval. If the informant was going to testify, we would have to move them out of the area after arrests were made. We could use

an informant over and over again if we were writing search warrants and hiding their identity.

We also used concerned citizens. We still had to check out their stories to confirm the information they were providing, but they were honest hard working people who either stumbled into information or noticed something their friend or neighbor was doing that they felt should be reported. This information was mainly used to obtain search warrants so they would not be identified or face retaliation.

Umatilla County was overrun with illegal aliens (Mexican nationals) dealing drugs. If they were not Mexican nationals they were connected to them. The Hermiston area was overwhelmed with pound dealers. Pendleton primarily had gram dealers. There were a few pound dealers in Pendleton and Milton-Freewater, but we did not hold a candle to Hermiston. Due to this fact we developed different strategies for working each area.

In general task-force members working in Pendleton could keep their statistics up on the number of suspects arrested. The task-force members in Hermiston were working on major drug dealers and were seizing large quantities of drugs and cash. This was the perfect marriage for the task force. As time went on, and to this day, I think the focus became the larger dealer and targeting suspects who can be prosecuted federally. As budgets grew tighter, federal money was needed to keep the task force running, and the pound dealer became the major target.

I will lay out some of the type of cases we were involved in during my time nineteen years with the Blue Mountain Enforcement Narcotics Team (BENT). I worked with over thirty police officers during that time, and I will not name any of those officers. In addition to the agencies I mentioned above, we worked with ATF, FBI, and DEA.

Our area was prime for major traffickers, as they could use the freeway system or would go south through the desert. One case we had information that a large shipment of cocaine was coming up through the desert. With the help of our patrol division, the vehicle was located. We seized over six hundred pounds of cocaine hidden in a false wall. The inside was three feet shorter than the outside. Who knows how many pounds of narcotics came to or through our area? It was not uncommon for a trafficker to send a woman and kids south to pick up a load of drugs to bring back to our area.

Concealment methods for transporting narcotics were amazing. Transporters would remove beds of trucks and replace them with false bottoms, build secret panels in doors and trunks, or fill gas tanks, spare tires, and dash boards with hidden compartments. We saw all these methods used.

//

Some of the cases we worked took months, so a search warrant could be over eighty pages long, all of our suspect and buy information had to be included. One such case took about four months. We used three informants and bought pounds of cocaine and guns.

Our main suspect Jorge lived in Milton-Freewater, Oregon. During our investigation, we identified thirteen other suspects. Due to the amount of drugs and the amount of money we would have to spend, we asked the ATF to join the case. With ATF on board, we also got the full weight of sentencing from the federal system. ATF was my favorite federal agency. I did not like their mission, but the agents were the best we ever worked with. Most ATF agents were prior law enforcement officers, so they understood how we operated.

When it came time to arrest the suspects, we had thirteen houses to execute search warrants. Which meant we had to draw up thirteen tactical plans. It took over a hundred federal, state, and local officers to execute the search warrants. There were so many officers and agents that we had to do the briefing in an airplane hangar. As it turned out, it was a big deal for ATF. Janet Reno (then attorney general) had to approve any raids where federal agencies were involved in. This was just after the raids in Waco, Texas, and Ruby Ridge over in Idaho.

Several of the suspects were a very dangerous. Two of them had been involved in shoot-outs in the streets of Milton-Freewater. One suspect pulled a gun on ATF agents as they executed the search warrant. He was subdued without a shot fired. It was a very successful day; we seized lots of cash, more guns, and drugs.

One suspect was not found that day. He managed to elude us for a couple of months but was caught crossing the border coming out of Mexico. Two of our suspects escaped custody in Portland. I really don't know how that happened, but one of them was later killed in the streets of Mazatlán.

I got permission for my son to ride along on this raid while we were executing the thirteen search warrants. One of our National Guard troops took him from one search warrant execution to another.

I thought it was important for him to see our operation up close and personal. I hoped it would help him understand what I did for a living. He knew how much fun I had at work, so I was a bit concerned he might consider law enforcement as a career. I never wanted him to be a cop. I was very happy when I learned he had received an ROTC scholarship to Oregon State University .

//

We almost always used women to help us buy narcotics during the Pendleton Roundup. Sometimes it was National Guard women or local women who were willing to help us.

With so many people in town the locals relaxed, and they felt safer selling narcotics to strangers.

A couple of buys stood out only because they ended in foot pursuits and fights. The women had strict orders to blend into the crowd when we approached the suspects.

One such buy was made in front of a local tavern. There were two suspects involved in the delivery. We had picked up a PRCA bull rider who liked the women we were with and had followed us from bar to bar, dancing with the gals. He had no idea who we were until we were hollering, "Police!" and chasing suspects down the street.

Another detective and I grabbed a guy who had headed for the street. We got him cuffed and dragged back in front of the bar. I looked down the street, and one of the detectives had the second guy by the belt and was dragging him back as his head occasionally hit the sidewalk. The bull rider was beside himself; he wanted to come out every night and work with us.

With all the commotion the bar started to empty. To our benefit we had arrested several of the patrons, and none of them wanted any part of what we were dishing out. It made me feel good that we had made that kind of impression on them. A couple of them were calling us by our first names. I heard a couple people say, "Hey Mike, Can't you let them go?" It brought a smile to my face; I knew we were making an impact in their world.

While talking to one of the suspects later, he made some smart comment. I told him that my goal was to become the most hated person in the county. He looked at the other detective and said, "You better set your goals a little higher. You already reached that one!" He made my night.

The second buy was a little more risky. We were buying a fairly large quantity of methamphetamine, and it was coming in from the Hermiston area. We had set the buy up with a local dealer, but he did not have the quantity we wanted, so he had called his distributor. We knew the more we bought, the higher the risk would be for us.

As we moved in for the arrest, the suspects abandoned their vehicle. They could not drive anywhere during the Pendleton Roundup. I chased my guy toward Safeway and tackled him in the parking lot. I located a handgun and secured him with thumb cuffs. Thumb cuffs were light and painful if the suspect resisted. I had a citizen stand on my guy while I went to assist my partners, who were looking for the second suspect. I had another citizen call Pendleton PD to assist.

I got back to my suspect just as Pendleton PD arrived. The patrol officer had not noticed the thumb cuffs and was trying to cuff my suspect before removing them. The suspect was screaming like a stuck hog. The officer thought the suspect was resisting, but he was about to pull the suspects thumbs off. Thumb cuffs separate your wrists farther than regular handcuffs.

//

Our west-end partners had been working a deal to purchase a pound or two of methamphetamine from a guy named Jesus who lived in the Hermiston area. It seemed like one of the places the drug dealers liked to meet were crowded locations, where they could blend in if necessary. After several failed attempts, the deal was finally made. We had planned to arrest Jesus and his wife when they left the area in their vehicle. They went on to a grocery store.

Jesus had thousands of dollars in task force funds, so my partner and I went after him. We must have been quite a sight as we ran past the checkout stands wearing full tactical vests and carrying shotguns.

I found Jesus halfway down an isle; he confronted me, forcing me to knock him down. When his wife turned to run, I caught her by the purse pulling her off her feet. My partner arrived, and we escorted our suspects out of the door. No one in the store said a word. Oh yes, and they still had our buy money.

//

I cannot even begin to tell you how many search warrants my west-end partners wrote looking for a pound of cocaine or methamphetamine. We had been searching on one warrant for quite some time, but had not found the large stash of drugs we knew was there. One of my partners from the east side walked out in some sage brush and noticed a wilted plant. He got to digging and found a couple of pounds of cocaine buried about two feet down. I was amazed. It affirmed the fact that you cannot quit searching too early. These suspects had all the time in the world to think of places to hide drugs.

These guys seemed to hide the drugs very well, but when it came to hiding their money they were kind of sloppy. On more than one occasion, we found over $100,000 in shoe boxes in the closet. In their defense, they couldn't put it in the bank.

//

When I started thinking about all the places our suspects hid drugs, one suspect, Javier, stands out. We knew Javier was selling pounds of marijuana, and we knew where he would go to hide them. I guess he thought if the marijuana was not at his house, he would not get arrested.

One afternoon officers from BENT executed a search warrant on Javier. We found enough evidence to arrest him, but we did not find the pounds we were looking for. So we kidnapped Javier—well I guess it was not kidnapping since he was technically under arrest—and drove him to a remote area where we had seen him hide larger quantities of Marijuana.

Javier started taunting us. He must have thought we could not find his stash. Since I already knew where the marijuana was buried, I thought we could have some fun with the young detective. This was his first search warrant, and he had worked with us less than a week. When we reached the area, I told the young officer to get Javier out of the car and threaten to shoot him if he did not tell us where he had buried the marijuana.

The young detective looked at me in shock and went to grab Javier. He pulled Javier out of the car and told him he would shoot him if he did not tell us where the marijuana was buried. I was standing behind the young detective looking at Javier. I winked at Javier and smiled. Javier smiled at the young detective and said it is a good day to die. You should have seen the look on the young detective's face when he turned around, with an expression like *What now, do I have to shoot him?* I think Javier enjoyed the joke, at least until we dug up his stash.

//

Milton-Freewater Police Department (MFPD) was having trouble with a farm labor camp. It got to the point where they could not enter it alone. One night MFPD received a call for assistance made from the labor camp, and when the officer arrived the car was fire bombed.

I grew up in Milton-Freewater and thought it was unacceptable to turn over the labor camp to a mob. The first night we were there gunfire erupted. Apparently no one thought it was a big deal, because no one called the police. We continued to make drug buys until we had enough information to execute several search warrants.

My direct supervisor was gone so the station commander stopped in and asked what I was doing. I told him I was finishing up some search warrants and putting some raid plans together for the Milton-Freewater labor camp. He said that it would be too dangerous and he didn't want us to do it. I completely ignored him mainly because I thought he was kidding.

Later in the day I was putting together teams to assist me with the raid when the station commander came in and asked what I was doing. I told him I had gotten the search warrants signed and was putting together a raid plan. He got very defiant and said, "I told you it was too dangerous, you are not going to do the raid."

I completely lost it. After telling him he could not stop me from doing my job, I went on a personal attack that got very graphic. After he left the room I thought about what I had said and figured the next call I would get was going to come from district headquarters. I had forgotten about what had transpired when Sergeant Morris, the supervisor from Milton-Freewater walked in. I asked what he was up to. He said the station commander had called him and said that it would be his ass if I did a raid in the Milton-Freewater labor camp and something went wrong.

I assured him that I had all the bases covered so he pitched in and assisted me with the raid plans. We entered the labor camp with a small army. We hit four places at the same time and were very successful. We kept up the pressure on the labor camp from that time forward. The management at the labor camp assisted us with our efforts, and together we helped clean up the problem.

We were in Milton-Freewater a short time after the raids on the labor camp and were debriefing after another raid in the area, when MFPD heard there was a large crowd gathering near the basketball court in the labor camp and that one person had been stabbed.

Since we were in full raid gear, all we had to do was saddle up and grab our shotguns. BENT went with the MFPD to access the situation. There were at least a hundred people milling around. We talked to a couple of loud mouths, while MFPD conducted their investigation. From that time forward they understood that we would not turn the labor camp over to a group of thugs.

//

As officers transferred into the task force, they served as new faces in the local drug culture, allowing us to use them to accompany informants to strengthen our cases. In one such case we were using a young female informant. Todd was a new officer to narcotics, so we paired them up. Todd posed as her uncle due to the large discrepancy in age.

Our girl set up a buy and was trying to get the suspect to sell straight to her "uncle," Todd. We were having a hard time identifying our suspect, so we told her not to get into the vehicle, and we would stop the car after the suspect sold the drugs to Todd.

Of course things never went as planned. The suspect talked the young female informant into his vehicle. Todd approached from the driver's side and made the exchange. Todd gave us the signal that the deal had been made, and we started to move in.

I was on foot behind the vehicle when I saw Todd leaning into the driver's-side window. It appeared that Todd and the suspect were struggling. I heard the engine race, and the vehicle started to take off as Todd fell back onto the ground. I thought Todd had been shot or stabbed. The female informant was still in the vehicle. I brought my weapon up and started to shoot the driver at the same time the female informant attacked him and was wrestling him on the driver's side of the vehicle.

I yelled, "Police!" but the suspect continued. I then fired two shots into the air, but the suspect did not slow down so I put two rounds into the front tire. Officers in undercover vehicles moved into the area to cut off the suspect. The suspect's front tire was going flat, and he was trapped, so he stopped and gave up.

Now we had a shooting incident, and we would have to do extra reports and an investigation had to be done. This was not our first shooting incident, and I had shot at the vehicle with an unauthorized weapon, so everyone involved knew there would be an investigation. I had been issued a Walther .380 for undercover work; the Walther is a quality weapon, but with the lightweight bullets I could not have penetrated a pop can, so I had a backup weapon.

The task force members had tried several 9 mm pistols to use as backup weapons, and we all liked the Glock, so I bought one and I was carrying it. To the general public this may seem like no big deal, and it really was not. But police departments sweat vicarious liability cases. A bad guy would not care what gun I shot him with—well, he might have preferred a .380—but the Oregon State Police said you could only use weapons and ammo they had provided. At the time the state police were carrying Smith and Wesson .357 revolvers.

One of the officers suggested that we pick up all the 9 mm brass and fire the .380 a few times. It was a remote enough area no one would know. Now we were talking about taking a slap-on-the-hand offense and making it a conspiracy. I told them it was not big deal, and I would take my chances with the brass.

A month or two later the superintendent showed up to tell me what my punishment would be for using an unauthorized weapon. I came to work wearing my normal attire: a dirty, torn tee shirt and matching jeans. The station commander met me and said there was a note in my box telling me that I was to meet the superintendent today and should dress appropriately. It was too late for that.

The superintendent was sitting behind the lieutenant's desk, and the department's legal counsel was sitting on our side of the table. The lieutenant and I sat down and had some small talk. The superintendent did not seem to care how I was dressed; I think that was the lieutenant's idea.

The superintendent asked me what had happened that night. I said, "Well, boss, you know what happened, or you would not be here. If you expect me to beg, it's not happening."

I paused and smirked at the legal counsel; he started to chuckle along with the superintendent. The lieutenant looked like he had seen a ghost. The superintendent said, "I'm going to bust you back a step for a month. Now get out of here." I think violating the policy cost me fifty dollars. Had we lied and gotten caught I could have been fired.

As it turns out, there had been a witness. About a week after the shooting, I ran into a young man who ran the mini-mart across the street from where the shooting had taken place. He told me I had scared the crap out of him and that he was in the mini-mart with the lights off, closing up when he saw the commotion. He said when I started shooting, he hid and did not come out.

If that happened now someone would have filmed it. Then you would be on the Today Show, and without knowing the facts the cops would have been crucified by the media. I would hate to be a police officer today; the news media was bad enough when I was working. A lot of what we did was in the paper or on the local news, and they rarely ever got the story right. The press is very critical of the police and the way we do business. If the police handled the facts the way the news media does, we would never win a case, and we would lose our jobs.

//

We had a family of brothers in Pendleton who were in trouble from the time they left high school. I had contact with all of them at one time or another. Over at least fifteen years two of them had been sent to prison. The charges varied from different types of drug charges to weapons possession.

All the brothers were users and were unpredictable. Jim was probably the brother I had had the most contact with. We had been working a case involving associates of Jim and enough information to execute a search warrant.

Normally we liked to execute search warrants in the early morning hours for the element of surprise. For some reason we needed to execute this warrant right away. By the time we got the warrant signed and had our team assembled, it was getting late.

We did our raid briefing and planned to park down a dead end street and walk into the residence. As we got close, we saw a car idling in front of the house. All of a sudden the lights came on and the car came toward us. I crossed over to the center of the street and ordered the driver to stop. The car accelerated, so I started to move across, out of the way.

As I looked up I saw I was getting crowded into a solid six-foot fence. I took aim at the driver and fired a round. As Jim hit me, it drove my arm down, causing bullet to hit the hood in front of him. Jim, who was driving the car, had recognized me after years of contact and had tried to run me down. One of my partners shot Jim just after he saw me get hit. Jim's car came to a stop down the street. The force of the impact had spun me around in the air, and I landed on the far side of the car.

I sent two officers after Jim, and the rest of the team got restacked and executed the search warrant. The reason I mention this story was to show how focused our team was. We could have been in total disarray after the shooting, but everyone stayed focused and did their job.

I had trouble with my back for quite some time after the incident. I thought that people with back problems were pussies, until I hurt mine. I had broken two small bones that stabilize you spine. After a few months, it was more uncomfortable than disabling. But, I'm no longer as quick to judge someone who claims back injuries.

Jim recovered from his wounds and was sent to prison for attempted murder.

//

We were working in Umatilla buying a pound of methamphetamine from Victor. Victor had other suspects running counter surveillance all around us. I need to take a quick break and explain counter surveillance anytime we were involved in a buy involving a large quantity of narcotics. Drug dealers send people out to saturate the area, looking for police or anything out of the ordinary. These were normally paranoid people, but when they were selling thousands of dollars of narcotics, they had a very real chance of getting ripped off or arrested.

We bought the pound of methamphetamine from Victor then moved into arrest him. Victor was trapped on a spit in a marina surrounded by the Columbia River. Victor ran into the Columbia River, took our buy money from his waist, and threw it into the river. We tried to get to Victor, but he turned and swam into the marina. I would guess the water was thirty-four degrees at the time. I told Victor he was going to drown if he did not come back. The case officer cut Victor off across the marina, and as he turned around I could see he was already hypothermic. I threw him a post to hold onto but he did not reach for it and went under. Divers later recovered Victor and our money.

//

I could not tell you how many doors we (BENT) kicked in over the years, but it must have been in the hundreds. I'm not talking about our entry team or SWAT. I'm talking about BENT proper. We approached every search warrant execution the same. We had a briefing, a run-through of assignments, and a walk-through of the floor plan. Then we had an after-action briefing. An outsider might say we were very fortunate, but it was not a game, and we were not playing.

Without going into how we got our information or what we had to do to get certain types of warrants, some warrants required us to follow certain steps before they could be executed.

One such case was at an automobile repair shop in Hermiston. It was not a legitimate repair shop, but there were a lot of trashed cars inside and around the building. BENT was staged outside the business when a large amount of marijuana was delivered. We waited for about fifteen minutes and executed our warrant. Six to eight illegal aliens ran in all directions. My partner and I took down two suspects in the building, and the rest of the team chased suspects outside in the dark.

Upon entry we had several marked units with overheads activated parked in front of the building near the street. The front door had been destroyed and was hanging by one hinge. Both suspects had been cuffed without incident, and my partner was covering them. I told him I was going to clear a couple of vehicles that were parked in the shop.

As I walked around a vehicle, I came face to face with another suspect. We were in full raid gear with badges displayed, I ordered him to the ground but he turned to run. I reached out and grabbed his shoulder; he threw an elbow, from which I was able to duck; and I spun him to the ground. He hit the concrete floor hard. I believe he had a black eye and was missing some teeth.

After the dust settled, and we were interviewing suspects, we learned that the suspect who tried to hit me was the landlord. Apparently he saw the commotion and then panicked when confronted. He should have listened. The next day the landlord went to the local police department, which had just gotten a new police chief. No one on BENT had ever met him—not even his officer assigned to the task force.

Without any facts or knowledge of the case, the new police chief told the landlord he should sue us, which of course he did. I believed the State of Oregon offered to pay his dental bill and the case was dropped, but I never had any respect or use for that police chief. Since that time, karma took care of him, and he no longer holds that position.

//

After a day in court myself and three members of BENT were headed back to the office, when we received a phone call asking us to check out a local man who was distraught over his job. According to the report, he was gathering weapons and was headed to work to take care of the people he felt were responsible of his situation.

We were armed with our handguns and our fancy court clothes. We pulled into the area where the suspect lived and saw him loading weapons into a vehicle. We called in to report our findings and were told to stop him. They did not want to stop him on the road. The suspect lived on a dead end street so we were forced to drive by twice. I knew from his posture he did not mistake us for Mormon missionaries.

The suspect got behind the opened door of his vehicle as we entered his driveway. He was armed with an M-1 Grand (semiautomatic rifle) and had a pistol stuck in his belt. I noticed the suspect had a thousand yard stare; he seemed to be looking right through us. We got out of the vehicle, and I identified ourselves as police officers and showed him our badges. He said, "I do not recognize your authority." I knew from his demeanor and statement that the suspect meant business.

I tried several times to get the suspect to put down his weapons and talk to us. The suspect made a run for cover; we were already at maximum pistol range and he had a high powered rifle. As he started to get into a shooting position, I shot the suspect. The suspect was incapacitated, and we were able to secure his carload of weapons.

Incidents like this happen without warning or preparation. These are the kinds of calls a uniformed officer would normally receive. We normally got to prepare, have a raid plan, and wear protective gear. But you don't always have the luxury of planning, which is why training is so important.

//

BENT had been very successful at doing what we called, "roundups." We would bring in a new informant; make as many buys as possible; and then arrest a large group of people. We were starting to educate the local drug dealers; they did not want to sell drugs to someone they did not completely trust.

We had brought a new informant into Pendleton who was making a few buys, but he was not as productive as we would have liked. We decided we needed to find a way to make him seem trustworthy to our bad guys. We decided to set up a small marijuana grow in his basement. We talked to the district attorney, and it was agreed that we could go ahead with our plan.

We located some surplus grow lights and small marijuana plants we had recently seized but no longer needed for evidence. We decided to leave the grow in the informant's basement for about a month, so he could bring guests home and show them that he was truly a bad guy whom they could trust.

All went well for about a week. The Informant brought a couple of reluctant dealers to his place and shown them his grow. That was all he needed to gain their confidence. The buys began to pick up.

We got a frantic phone call from our informant, who told us that someone had broken into his place and stole the marijuana—grow lights and all. We only had two lights and about thirty plants, but they were ours, so we took the burglary very seriously. After all, we told the district attorney that we would keep a close eye on the operation.

Whether they knew it or not, the suspects had embarrassed BENT, and we would not tolerate that. We pulled out all the stops and found a suspect who had the plants from our marijuana grow. We put significant pressure on him until he ratted out the person who had committed the burglary. He was also able to show us where the lights and shields had been dumped.

This suspect took us to a very secluded area of the county, about thirty miles south of Pendleton. Armed with everything but a confession from our burglary suspect, I grabbed a new member of BENT and picked up the suspect. The suspect was known to me; he had given us some information in the past so he was not too surprised that we asked him to jump in our car and go for a ride with us.

I could see the stress in his face as we drove out of town and turned off on a side road a few miles from where he had dumped our grow. I could not tell him we had lost our marijuana grow, so I started talking about a burglary on the south hill, where our informant lived. I asked the suspect what he knew about the burglary; his mouth was so dry he could hardly talk.

When I got to the spot where the evidence had been dumped, I jammed on the brakes, sliding to a stop. I jumped out and jerked the door open and grabbed the suspect. Before I could drag him to the edge of the road overlooking the evidence, he broke down and confessed to the burglary.

I think I scared the new detective as badly as I did our suspect. Since I just wanted to save face with the district attorney, we recovered our marijuana growing operation and never filed any charges on the two suspects. Both of them felt like they owed us for quite some time.

Sometimes we thought a little too far outside the box. It could have been a real embarrassment if we had not located the suspects or our marijuana growing operation.

//

Not all undercover operations put us at great risk. I had bought heroin from Miguel in Walla Walla, Washington, and had convinced him to bring heroin to a small park at the southwest corner of Main and Court Streets, where Hamley's restaurant now sits.

We had a criminal meeting prior to lunch, so there were about fifteen detectives and narcotics officers there who wanted to watch the buy. While I was waiting in the park, a friend of mine walked by and wanted to chat. I had to tell him I was working. Miguel arrived right on time and sold me the heroin. Miguel's only comment was that he did not know there was much demand for heroin in Pendleton.

He was right; I wanted to get some heroin to enter on our end-of-the-month report. Had anything gone wrong or required a takedown, there were probably about fifteen detectives close enough to grab

Miguel within seconds. There may not have been enough of Miguel left to take to jail.

Actually, the more cops you have on a guy, the more likely one of the cops will get hit by another cop. I once broke a cop's nose when he ran up behind me to jump on a guy. Just as I cocked my arm back to hit the suspect, my elbow met his nose. I once had a chunk taken out of my arm by an officer who was swinging handcuffs at a suspect's wrist, and I got in the way.

//

On a nice summer morning I received a call from our BENT partners in Hermiston; they needed assistance with a one-pound methamphetamine buy in their area. The transaction was set for early afternoon. After we met and received our assignments, we learned that we would be purchasing the methamphetamine through a local suspect, but the connection was coming out of the Tri-Cities, Washington. This was not uncommon; we worked cased with the task forces in Yakima, Washington and the Tri-Cities, Washington on a regular basis. Borders meant nothing to drug dealers.

As drug deals go, it was run of the mill: people get nervous, so times and locations change. During this negotiation process, we noticed the same vehicle and suspect was showing up and driving around each location. This lookout or counter surveillance suspect was doing the same thing we were; he was looking for anything out of the ordinary.

The negotiations continued until around 9:30 p.m., and the final location ended up being the Wal-Mart parking lot in Hermiston. As the deal was going down, and the team started to move in to take off the suspects, I saw the vehicle and suspect who had been working counter surveillance all day move into the parking lot. This suspect pulled into a parking stall about ten stalls from where the deal was going down.

97

I warned the takedown team and started moving toward the counter surveillance suspect, so we could grab everybody at the same time. When I got to the driver's door, the window was down, and I saw a .45-caliber pistol in his hand. Since he was looking in the other direction it was easy to get the advantage on the suspect. When my partners moved in to take down the main suspect, I identified myself to the counter surveillance suspect. He never even turned to look at me, and after a few seconds, he laid the pistol in the seat. Most of these guys claimed to not understand English, but we had no problem communicating that night.

//

Narcotics operations always puts the officers who work them in the gray areas of law enforcement, but you always hope that your own department will stand behind you and get the facts before they believe the worst. I stated in the beginning that there would be some people I will mention who should not reflect badly on the OSP, and the following story includes one of those people.

Don't get the impression that I am trying to paint myself as some kind of saint. I would step over any line you put in front of me. I liked working in the gray areas; it required creativity. I would not break the law or lie. If I got caught doing something, I had no problem riding the heat.

One afternoon I was in the office when a supervisor from another area stopped by and told me one of our old informants was in possession of a handgun. They had discovered it while searching his vehicle prior to a controlled drug buy.

The supervisor showed me the handgun he had seized from the informant. I wondered what this had to do with me. The supervisor then gave me the handgun like it was a gift; no paperwork or explanation as to why I was getting the handgun. I had a witness, but it made me nervous enough that I documented the transaction in my notebook and told several people what had happened. I then locked it in a temporary holding area, where I keep narcotics funds. A guy never knows when he will need some insurance.

A few months later the same supervisor who had given me the handgun showed up in Pendleton one evening and asked me to meet him at his motel. When I arrived he told me he was looking into my BENT partners on the west side. It had to do with how some computers were purchased. It seemed like an administrative issue rather than something that warranted an investigation.

The supervisor told me that if I stay out of this investigation, he would make me a sergeant. He wasn't even coy about the offer. First of all he did not have that kind of power, and I was already on the sergeants list and had decided I did not want to take a sergeant position for several reasons.

I had not trusted this supervisor since he gave me the handgun. I left the motel and warned every member of BENT that the supervisor from headquarters was looking into our operation. My partners laughed it off until Internal Affairs (IA) started poking around. The investigation lasted several weeks. I had IA trying to run me down to interview me. I was successful at avoiding them, until I went to a conference in Portland and they tracked me down.

The whole thing was starting to piss me off, so I called the deputy superintendent and told him what I knew about the background of the supervisor conducting the investigation. I also told him the investigation was some kind of witch hunt to cover his tracks. When I told him about the handgun, he ordered me to turn it over to IA. The deputy superintendent told me that this was the end of all this.

I think one of the detectives transferred over the frustration of the case, but there was nothing done that would have justified the investigation.

As it turned out the supervisor had a hand in some of the events that lead to the investigation. This is why I have mentioned several times how important it is to always cover your ass. We had done nothing wrong; someone in headquarters perceived a problem, so we all had to endure an investigation. As I recall, this supervisor had put himself in charge of the investigation, because he had something to do with one of the computers in question.

Again one bad apple should not reflect on the whole department, but you need to get them out before they spoil the bin.

GIVING COPS A BAD NAME

BEFORE I TELL SOME stories about these detectives, especially from other agencies, you need to realize that back in those days a lot of small departments did not have the resources to do thorough background investigations on some of these officers. At the time, most departments did not have a lot of manpower and did not want to lose one of their good officers to a narcotics operation. This is opposite of what should have occurred.

We needed the best officers. Narcotics officers had a lot of freedom and very little supervision in those days. You wanted the officer with the best work ethic, the highest morals, no financial or marriage problems, and great judgment, as well as a guy who could think on his feet. Narcotics work is fluid and requires innovative thinking. The world of narcotics is ever changing, which forced us to stay current with all types of criminal activity and case law.

I mentioned smaller departments as having officers you would consider loose cannons. Don't think for a minute that the Oregon State Police did not hire people who later showed extremely poor judgment, and should have never been put into an undercover position. Not everyone is cut out for undercover work.

//

In one case I found an officer from another department had lied on a search warrant. I had a nagging question about him, so I made a call to his old department and found out he was suspected of stealing property from them and was terminated.

I contacted his department and told them what he had done and what I had learned. The administrator called in his lieutenant and asked him about the background check on the detective. The lieutenant said he had not had time to get it done. The detective was terminated the next day. Officers like this are a black eye to all law enforcement. We do police our own.

//

I was working with Jim, a police officer from a Pendleton; his administration was good enough to let him go with me to anther jurisdiction to work a couple of undercover cases. The chief of police in the community where we were working lent us his detective, Tom to cover Jim and the informant while we were in town.

I had already made some contacts in a local bar and went to hang out for a while and get to know some more of the locals. After a couple of hours I went back to where I had last seen Jim. I found Tom the local officer, who was tasked with watching Jim passed out in his car. There were beer bottles all over the front seat. I drove around until I located Jim's vehicle. I started jumping into back yards and peeking into windows until I located Jim and the informant.

We later learned that Tom's wife had just left him, which was no excuse. The next time we came to the area we were told that Tom's issues had been worked out and he was sent to us again. We decided that we would send Tom in with the informant to witness the buy. I thought that even with his history he could stand in the corner, watch the deal, and report his observations back to us. The informant was searched and given the money for a quantity of cocaine and away they went.

We met at a predetermined location and were given a quantity of coke significantly less than what we had paid for. As we jumped the informant about the amount of cocaine we received for our money, he pointed to Tom and said he snorted it. Tom's comment chilled me to the bone. He said, "a man's got to do what a man got to do."

I testified against Tom at his dismissal hearing. And we threw our case out against the suspect.

These were isolated incidents over twenty-eight years, but these are the kind of stories that give police officers a bad name—especially narcotics officers.

//

A lot of people asked how you can work undercover and not use dope. If you are posing as a low-lever addict or dealer, it's a little harder not to use in front of the dealer. Most users can't wait to get whatever they are buying into their system. You need a good cover story if you are not using; it could be as simple as a job interview in the morning with a urine test or an appointment with your probation officer.

I took in a cigar and a beer into most houses when I was making a buy. It made it easier for them to pass the joint or crack pipe around me if my hands were full. If you were buying larger quantities, they usually assumed you were in for the money. Small amounts for coke or meth-amphetamine could be for the "bag bitches", these were gals that would do anything for a bag of meth or coke.

I never used drugs, but I did simulate a few times if there was no way out. For example, I always kept a gum wrapper handy. You could run a straw past a line of coke if you kept the mirror or glass plate in your lap or away from the suspect and use your hand to pull the powder off the edge of the glass and into the gum wrapper in your hand then you crushed the wrapper and put it in your pocket for evidence.

I did this in front of an informant one time who was sitting next to me he thought I did a line, until he saw me give the gum wrapper to my partner. I guess if I had a gun to my head I may have done a line, but it was never necessary in my career.

Actually buying dope was no big deal. Any low-life addict can buy dope. The trick to buying dope was to figure out a way to do it in a safe manner and not have to use it. It was not worth my health or my career to make a case. I will admit that I might have been an adrenaline junky, but I had other outlets to get my fix.

MARIJUANA GROWS

We found Marijuana grows on public land, private land, buried under ground, in crop circles, in hay stacks, in old barns, and in homes. They were everywhere. The Oregon National Guard helicopter crews partnered with law enforcement throughout Oregon and used us as spotters, looking for marijuana grows every summer.

At one time the National Guard could fly in, drop, rope, and sling out the plants to save us from hauling them out on our backs. We tried using the Chinooks with a basket, but between the three-hundred-pound basket flying around and trees snapping off, it was too dangerous as the rotor wash was tremendous.

One flight was up Hell's Canyon on a hot day. We flew from the river up into a boxed canyon and lost our lift. The blades started popping, and the chopper started falling tail first. The pilot did a great job. As the chopper was falling, the pilot flopped the chopper over on its side and pointed it toward the river. There were not doors on the chopper so the guys on the bottom were looking at the canyon floor coming up quickly. I was looking at the sky, so it was less traumatic for me. I have to say I could hear them screaming like school girls over the noise of the chopper. We never talked about that trip much, and fewer guys volunteered to fly after that.

//

We went to the Snake River in Wallowa County. Deputies had been monitoring John's activities and knew he had a marijuana-growing operation up Cherry Creek. We used two jet boats; one was operated by our fish and game department. We were about a mile from Cherry Creek when we came around the bend of the river and saw John standing near his jet boat. He started to make a run for his boat as we came along side.

We must have looked like pirates ready to board. John had three rifles pointed at him, he made the right move and gave up without incident. His boat contained marijuana that he had already harvested. We did not have another boat captain, so we were forced to let John drive his own boat out of the area to be seized. This was rough country. We spent the rest of the day pulling and destroying marijuana plants.

//

We received information from Pam that there was a large area that had been cleared in the forest, and there were thousands of small plants in pots about four miles above her cabin. My partner and I hiked into the area the next morning guided by the Pam. As we approached the area where the potted plants were, we saw marijuana and heard voices. We sent Pam back to call the rest of our team and tell them we had a marijuana growing operation and suspects.

My partner and I laid in wait until the suspects drew close enough for us to overwhelm them. After subduing the two suspects and securing them and their weapons, we went to look for the rest of the crew. We did not find anyone else in the canyon; they were either alone or had run off. Since there was no way to get into the area, and we had no way to communicate, we walked the suspects out of the canyon before dark.

//

Our counterparts in Union County had discovered a marijuana grow in a huge haystack. This was in a very remote area. The ranch they had purchased had no cattle but lots of hay. Apparently someone had seen the suspects going in and out of the haystack. There was a stolen, commercial generator on wheels, near the haystack.

After an investigation, the detectives in Union County were able to obtain a search warrant. We set a raid plan in motion. My job was to clear the haystack with half the entry team, while the other half secured the cabin.

As I entered the haystack it was lit up like a ball park; marijuana plants were everywhere. I took about five steps into the grow, yelling, "Police search warrant!" when the lights went out. I expected that gunfire would follow. I continued to yell and move forward with my light. We cleared the grow without incident and later learned that the timer on the generator had shut off the lights just as we entered. That made it a little more exciting than it needed to be.

//

We found several underground and undercover grows. This seemed to be a natural progression due to the pressure we were exerting by flying for grows. At the time, power companies would tell us if they had someone diverting (stealing) power or using excessive amounts of power. As time passed, so did this practice as companies were afraid that they would get sued for giving us information.

One such case took us to Milton-Freewater. The power company had found a house that had bypassed the meter and after some follow-up investigation, we obtained enough information for a search warrant.

When we executed the search warrant, we found the marijuana grow and evidence that the Hell's Angels were involved. We never found the suspects, but someone had left his colors (his vest that identified him and his membership as a Hell's Angel). To possess a set of colors without being a member of the Hell's Angels could cost you your life.

//

While doing our marijuana-eradication flights, one of our spotters located a large marijuana grow on USFS property in a remote area of Umatilla County. We snuck into the area with a four-man team and located a marijuana grow that was over 10,000 plants. There were a growing number of marijuana-growing operations tended by illegal aliens.

The amount of work and equipment involved in these grows was staggering. In this case over a mile of pipe was laid, and it ran up the canyon where there was good water flow. They could then run the pipe down the canyon, off the canyon floor, where there was no water and set up an irrigated grow with a drip system so they would not have to pack water.

We did not locate any suspects on our approach; we set up an observation point close to the grow and monitored it for several days. We were assisted by investigators from the USFS. We finally took a day and moved back into the marijuana grow for a day to wait for someone to return. We saw a bear working the area and chewing up drip line, but the suspects never returned.

While we were hiding in the brush, my partner and I heard movement in the leaves I looked above us and saw a rattle snake coming to use our hideout. I found out my partner did not like snakes, but he still did his part. While I pinned it down, he was able to cut the head off. About a half hour later, the head was laying there with the mouth open so I took a stick to touch the fangs. The mouth snapped shut on the stick and venom dripped out of the fangs. If we had played with it we could have been bitten by a dead snake.

While following up on a lead regarding a marijuana grow south of Baker, my partner and I contacted a suspect in a camp and found a fifty-five gallon drum with five or six big rattlers. I can only assume his intention was to dump the rattle snakes when the cops arrived. I guess we got to him before he got to the snakes.

//

This has nothing to do with marijuana grows but in the late 1990s we were having trouble with the Asians moving in during the mushroom-picking season. Gunfire was erupting. They would be picking on USFS land and claim an area for themselves. If someone came to pick in that area they would run them off, Fish and Wildlife officers worked most of these cases.

One year a buyer was shot and killed in Wallowa County. The Wallowa County Sheriff's Office contacted us and asked if we would be willing to work there, posing as mushroom pickers. Three of us went to an area that had burned the year before and picked a few mushrooms and monitored activity in the area for a couple of days. We were never able to make any criminal cases.

I mention this not to scare people out of the woods, but to demonstrate that the two-legged critters in the woods can be worse than the four-legged ones. I would always be aware of your environment while enjoying USFS land.

//

Since we were putting a lot of pressure on outdoor grows, they started moving back into houses. One such grow was in a house in a secluded area of the Blue Mountains. We had reliable information from an informant regarding a marijuana grow and had additional information confirming information received by the informant.

The last step was to fly to the house in the middle of the night using Forward Looking Infrared (FLIR). I signed up for the flight and met the pilots at the airport. The pilots warned me if I looked into the FLIR for too long, I could get sick. I loved flying with the helicopter crew and had never felt sick. We soon got over our target east of Weston in the Blue Mountains and started making passes. I confirmed the existence of what appeared to be a large heat source and a dog standing outside. Then I noticed I was feeling a little nauseous I looked away from the machine for a while and started feeling normal. I guess those boys knew what they were talking about.

Based on all of our information I wrote a search warrant. From the surveillance we had done, both on foot and from the air, it was going to be a dangerous place to hit because they could see us coming from a great distance.

I decided I would go in posing as a bear hunter and get permission to hunt the nearby canyon, which I did. While talking to the suspects about bear hunting I was able to meet two of them. The plan was going to be to have people stationed in the forest and a helicopter on standby then drive in and knock on the door again. Since they had seen my van and met me they should not raise suspicion.

Things never work out as planned. Before we left, the perimeter team called and said at least one guy was in the woods using a chainsaw. This would not change our plan. We had the helicopter and a perimeter team to corral any suspects outdoors. I was responsible for getting the guy to the door, jerking him out, and covering him while the entry team came out of the van to secure the house.

I drove up with the team and knocked on the door as planned. The guy who opened the door was huge—at least 6'3" and six hundred pounds. I had a job to do, so I stuck my right arm under his left arm pit and reached up with my left hand, so I could lock them together for leverage. I started moving him out of the doorway toward the edge of the porch as the team started exiting the vehicle. One of our big guys was almost crushed by this guy as he launched off the porch.

As the dust settled and people were being rounded up, I looked at my suspect. He apparently had a severe case of diabetes. His legs were black. When he hit the ground, they burst open like watermelons. We called an ambulance to transport him to a local hospital for treatment. He was so heavy it took six of us to get him loaded into the ambulance. He must have pleaded guilty. I never saw him again nor heard what had happened to him.

ENTRY TEAM

THE DISTRICT IV ENTRY Team responded to major cases in a large geographical area. District IV went from east of Bend, Oregon, to the Idaho border; south to California; and north to Washington. I believe the entry team existed for about five years until they were disbanded due to budget cuts and the expansion of the OSP SWAT team. We did cross-train with the OSP SWAT team in Eastern Oregon on a couple of occasions. On large raids the entry team could provide a perimeter team.

Working narcotics is a team sport. If another agency, area, or task force called, we all responded. We were doing so many high-risk entries that Sergeant Ray Berryman established a District IV entry team. We were not SWAT —we did not have the equipment or training that a SWAT team would have.

Sergeant Berryman had served in Vietnam and stayed very active in the Army reserves. He ended his military career as command sergeant major for the Oregon National Guard. Without Sergeant Berryman, we would not have had an entry team or the training to keep us safe.

We did train three or four times a year working on marksmanship, stress scenarios, mock entries, physical fitness testing, and team-building exercises like repelling. When we met to execute a search warrant, we would do briefings and dry runs on floor plans. After the search-warrant executions, we would do after-action briefings. We had an extremely disciplined team. Every team member did his job and did it well.

I don't want to make it sound like we had no special equipment for officer safety; we had tactical vests, helmets, and assistance from the Oregon National Guard. They could provide helicopters, some equipped with FLIR capabilities and LAVs (Lightweight Assault Vehicles) an eight-wheel drive floating tank without guns. We used LAV's on all the entries where we could justify it. In the mountains you could drive down a road at forty-five miles an hour where a four-by-four pickup could do about twenty miles per hour. I saw an OSP Fish and Wildlife pickup try to keep up with us on one search warrant execution at one point I could see the underside of the pickup, he was forced to back off.

A lot of Eastern Oregon is remote, and that is where we spent our time due to that fact that the criminal element likely thought there was no law enforcement presence in the area or if there was, Barney Fife would show up.

//

One of these groups was affiliated with the Hell's Angels. They set up a huge methamphetamine lab in a remote area west of the Wallowa Mountains. A neighbor reported suspicious activity and chemical fires that burned with unusual colored flames. After an investigation by members of a task force working in the Union County area, enough information was obtained for a search warrant.

There was a house and a lab to clear, so we needed three teams: a perimeter team, a lab-entry team, and an entry team for the house. The house sat at the base of a mountain. About two hundred feet above the road, there was a long, winding road up to the house, so the suspects could see a vehicle coming up the driveway. Due to the layout of the property, about half the team, including the perimeter team, hiked into the area. One team drove up the driveway announcing our presence after the other teams were set.

The lab team was just entering the lab, and the rear guard was watching the back of the house, when shots were heard from inside the house. Just as the lab team was entering the lab, the back door of the house opened and out stepped a naked man pointing a handgun at team members. The suspect was shot, and the lab was secured. This was one of the largest labs we ever recovered. They had 5,000 ml vessels and heating mantles, so they could cook batches of methamphetamine the size of basketballs. The suspect died from injuries sustained during the gun battle.

The members of the entry team showed a lot of discipline that day. No one got distracted by the gunfire in the house or when the suspect came outside. We trusted the people we had watching our backs, and the perimeter team to keep us safe while we completed our assigned tasks. Thanks to Sergeant Berryman's training, everyone did their job.

//

The week after the shooting in Union County, we had a search warrant to execute in Umatilla County. Of course the shooting was fresh on everyone's minds. This warrant was being executed on a mobile home. Mobile homes are very dangerous to clear due to the long hallways with no cover. As I came to the room at the end of the hallway, a figure appeared in the dark doorway and would not respond to my commands.

As I got to the doorway I kicked the person in the chest and entered the room. After clearing the room, my partner cuffed the suspect. It was then I realized I had kicked a woman the chest sending her into the far wall. When the suspect did not respond, the officers behind me thought I was going to shoot. I was focused on the suspect's hands and never saw a weapon. I took a lot of grief about kicking an old lady in the chest.

//

We were working a case involving a local informant who was getting up to ten pounds of methamphetamine at a time from an areas south of Portland, Oregon, in Wilsonville. We did several buys and obtained enough information for search warrants in Wilsonville and Umatilla County. We used our entry team and developed a raid plan. At most locations the raids went well. We seized twenty-one pounds of methamphetamine, a couple of pounds of cocaine, and cash.

At one residence the suspect was in the shower. When he heard the announcement of, "Police search warrant!" he grabbed his guns that were with him in the shower. The first kick of the bathroom door must have hit him. The door bounced back and was kicked again. This time the door and the suspect went flying. Guns and methamphetamine were scattered in the bathroom. Another near-catastrophe was avoided by being fast and violent.

I say "fast and violent" for a reason. We have to be fast enough to be safe, so suspects would not have time to grab a gun, hide, or barricade themselves in a room. We have to be violent enough so they will comply;

all suspects are given a warning to get down. If they do not get down they, are put down. If an officer pauses, he would have the rest of the team stacked up behind him, and we would not be able to secure the residence.

//

I do not tell this story to embarrass anyone but to show why it is import-ant to get new officers up to speed as soon as possible. Our task force partners in Hermiston had been working on a suspect dealing pounds of methamphetamine. A search warrant was obtained and a raid plan developed. I would be entering the house with a new task-force officer. This young man was as good an officer as any I ever worked with, but he had not trained with us long.

We approached the first bedroom to the left of the front door. As we entered the bedroom I went right which meant he was going to clear everything left of the door. The only problem was that there was a na-ked woman on the bed, and she was on the right side of the room. My young partner was drawn to her like a moth to a flame. I rolled back to the left and found our main suspect hiding behind the door. Of course he did not want to give up right away.

I never had to say a word; my young partner hung his head and apolo-gized profusely. It was not his fault. After you train enough, you learn to react to different scenarios. He was a quick study and ended up being one of the best tactical officers on the team. I never worried about him after that day: lesson learned.

//

Not all of our entries were fast and violent. We had a suspect who had explosives, booby traps, Rottweiler's, and automatic weapons. One of the automatic weapons was pointed down a long exposed driveway.

During the raid planning, it was decided that we would create a ruse to lure the suspect from the house.

The suspect had a yacht at the Marina in Umatilla, Oregon. Detectives had the marina call and tell the suspect his yacht was on fire. As the suspect drove to the marina we were able to arrest him without incident. This case was prosecuted in federal court. I believe he defense was that he was in the CIA. He was convicted. I guess the jury did not believe him either.

//

My normal assignment on the entry team was as the point man— meaning the first person through the door after it had been forced open. I don't know how that evolved, but I may have felt safer in this role. I had read that it was the second or third officer through the door that was most likely to get shot.

Our entry team was called to assist detectives in another county. I had a young officer who wanted to go first into a twenty-four-foot, travel trailer in a compound where we had already cleared several structures. The first thing I told him was that if he fell down I was going to run over him. Of course he tripped, I waited for him to regain his footing, and we continued toward the trailer. As we approached, a deputy from another agency was near the trailer and jumped in front of us. Now instead of first in line, I was third in line.

As you could guess, it was so narrow we were forced to turn sideways with all our gear on. There was a small bedroom at the end of the hall-way. The deputy entered the room and stepped a little to the right so I could just see over the young officer's shoulder. What I saw chilled me to the bone. The suspect was laying on his right side facing away from us.

There was a pistol in his right hand. When the detective entered the room, the suspect started rolling over pistol in the air. The suspect held the pistol on the deputy, and I had no shot. The suspect hesitated then lowered the pistol. This may have only taken five seconds, but it seemed like an eternity.

After the suspect had been secured, I confronted the deputy. First of all he had ignored the instructions during the raid briefing. Our team was assigned to clear the area; his job was to watch the perimeter. Since I did not work with him, I had to let it go, but he had put our lives in danger. If the suspect had shot we had no choice but to advance into gunfire, because the deputy would have been wounded and trapped in the room.

While I was taking my pound of flesh from the deputy, he told me the reason he did not shoot was because he had arrested the guy before and knew he would not shoot him. He took a huge risk with our lives, and it worked out.

//

I first heard the term "to overwhelm" a suspect used by a German national police officer who talked to us during a training session at Camp Rilea. She was telling us how they overwhelm suspects who may or may not have given up after a critical incident. When asked to define the term, she smiled and said they beat the crap out of them. Whether you call it overwhelming them or subduing them with speed and violence to gain the advantage, I think we are talking about the same thing.

To illustrate my point, we were executing an early-morning search warrant in the Hermiston area. We had been buying methamphetamine from the suspect, so we were executing this warrant with all the speed and violence we could muster.

After gaining entry Mike Schultz and I headed down the hall toward the first bedroom. The door was closed, but we could hear a drawer open and what sounded like a gun being slapped around inside it, without hesitating we kicked the door. The suspect had his hand in the dresser drawer trying to secure a .45 caliber pistol. Between our speed and all the commotion of doors crashing and us yelling, the suspect got so excited he could not get a grip on the pistol. Mike and I were able to overwhelm the suspect before he got a grip on the gun. Our fast and violent action saved his life and maybe our own.

SWAT

WHEN THE SPECIAL WEAPONS and Tactics Team (SWAT) was established, all the members were required to live and work within a couple of hours of Salem. I would never have admitted it at the time, but I truly wanted to join the team.

Reg Madsen was a young, dynamic trooper who was a counter sniper on the SWAT. He asked for and received a transfer to Baker City in Eastern Oregon. After he got settled into the area he called me and asked if I wanted to be his SWAT observer and counter-sniper, he said the department was willing to establish an eastern Oregon team perimeter team. I was forty-two at the time and I knew this would be my last shot to be a member of the OSP SWAT, I told him I would do it.

Just a note about Reg Madsen, Reg was a guy who always made you smile. Reg went through some personal tragedies while I knew him, but he always showed a positive upbeat side that make you feel good when you were around him.

Even when Reg was diagnosed with cancer he continued to bring joy to people. While Reg was fighting his own cancer he was the Oregon Chapter President for Bikers Fighting Cancer. During that time he sponsored a boy with terminal stomach cancer. Over the three years

Reg was fighting cancer he organized a group of us who would ride our bikes to Baker City and hang out on the Harrell ranch for three days as his guest.

Reg Madsen retired a Lieutenant with the Oregon State Police in LaGrande, Oregon. Reg's assignments included SWAT, MRT, Undercover Narcotics, Criminal Division and he worked in the patrol division.

Reg was a veteran of the United States Military. He was an Army Paratrooper and Military Police officer. He lived by the Moto: "It's All Good. No Worries." Reg lost his fight to cancer at the age of forty-four.

I want to publicly thank the Harrell clan from Baker City for welcoming us into their homes and treating Reg's friends like family. While we were at the Harrell ranch Reg's mother-in-law and sisters-in-law would bring us breakfast. Reg's brothers-in-law would come by to make sure we had what we needed for our camp.

Rick Giestwhite the SWAT commander called to see if I was serious about joining the SWAT team. He laid out all the reasons it may not work. Rick and I had worked together when I was a recruit in Eugene.

Rick insulted me by asking if I could pass the SWAT physical. In his defense he knew I had major knee reconstruction the year before. I had been wrestling in the World Police and Fire Games in Memphis and blew out my knee, at forty-one years old I should have known better. The upside was the best knee Doctors in the United States saw me and agreed to put me back together. I had followed the doctor's orders and felt the knee was good as new, maybe better. The doc had cleaned out all the normal wear and tear from years of running and working out. I worked out nearly every morning with members of the Blue Mountain Enforcement Narcotics Team so I knew the physical fitness test would be not a problem.

Rick said he would be there in the morning to give Reg and me the physical fitness test. After the Physical Fitness test Rick continued to tell me how difficult it would be to travel that far for training and callouts. I felt like he was trying to make me beg, but I finally wore him down. Rick told me I was on the team as long as I passed a psychological exam, now that made me sit up and take notice.

I really did not know if I could pass a Psych test, I was a bit radical. I was unsympathetic and showed almost no compassion for anyone I dealt with. The dreaded day arrived I left Pendleton at three in the morning. I had a 6:30 a.m. appointment with the shrink in Portland.

He started out with a few pictures, one sticks in my mind. The Doc showed me a picture of a guy who was in a disheveled suit putting on a tie, a woman was on the bed with one arm hanging off. She looked like she had been raped and killed. He asked me what I saw in the picture I said it looks like the woman is exhausted and the husband or boyfriend is getting ready for work and trying to let her get some sleep.

That was the order of the day I minimized and lied about everything he asked me. I almost forgot the ink blots, all of them looked like butter fly's a few looked like bats. Then the written, test there were over five hundred questions. I'm no genius but even I can remember how I answered a question a couple of hours before.

A week later I found out I must be the best liar in Oregon I had passed the psych test. I think the brass may give me the opportunity to join SWAT because they never dreamed I could pass the Psych test.

The training was a dream come true. We did a lot of training at Camp Rilea on the Oregon Coast near Seaside. Sometimes we would be qualifying with rifles and pistols so we would be shooting for two or three days straight. Who cared if it was raining or the wind was blowing, we were still shooting and getting paid for it, I loved it.

SWAT to me was being part of a brotherhood of like-minded guys taking on a task. I had as much fun at training as I did on operations. How many people get to shoot as much as they want; shoot from helicopters; practice their long range hunting shots; rappel out of Black Hawk Helicopters, rock climb; run confidence courses and snatch and grabs; and practice hunting skills and camouflage techniques. The Oregon State Police had very good training officers assigned to SWAT, but they were not afraid to bring in experts or to send us off to train or to a school.

SEAL Team 2 worked with us on stressed shooting. Instead of shooting from known positions and ranges, they would have us run down range and tell us to shoot on a downhill slope where it was hard to get into comfortable shooting positions. They covered techniques as simple as cleaning your weapon to prolong their use. A lot of us used copper brushes to clean our rifle barrels, they suggested other methods. And they were great guys.

The Sixth Army Group came to Camp Rilea and worked with us on tactical entries. We had a German tactical commander talk to us about their mission and how they handled tactical situations in their country. Some of our team went to train in Los Angeles with LA County SO and LAPD officers.

One of my bomb-squad partners and I were sent to a nationally recognized explosive entry school at Gunsite in Prescott, Arizona.

The vicarious liability of police officers is extreme. It is a lot cheaper to spend time and money on a police officer than to try to explain to a civil court why an officer had not been trained in a certain area. Even if an officer misses an intended target, and it is later learned that he could not qualify with his handgun, there is a potential law suit. Maintaining training records is important. I documented every class I ever went to or taught. I had over 4,300 hours of specialized training.

Training reinforces one of the SEAL mottos: two in one and one is none. Meaning, you can't count on your gear if you only have one radio battery, and if it dies or goes bad, you may no longer be an asset to the mission. It makes you look at all your gear and think about what may go wrong.

You practice every possible scenario in training. You can get the gear down; you can get the lingo down; you can get the moves down; but you will never know if you are truly ready until you are deployed.

We occasionally trained with Portland SWAT. We had great scenarios and sometimes used civilian actors. We used aircraft at the Portland airport and trains at the train station to practice hostage rescue. At times we used paint bullets this made you a bit more vigilant. The paint bullets did hurt if they caught bare skin or a knuckle. Training officers attempted to make training as real as possible, but it was still training.

Sometime around 1996 Portland SWAT and OSP SWAT trained with the FBI's Hostage Rescue Team (HRT) at the Portland International Airport. FBI's HRT is not to be confused with the regional FBI's SWAT. They are both part of the FBI's Critical Incident Response Group.

The FBI's HRT and SWAT have some of the best training, gear, and facilities in the world. At the time of the training one of the agents told me that the FBI's HRT had not been used on an actual mission. Until you test your skills in real-world situations you don't know how good you are. Remember this was a historical observation before 9-11; I'm sure this is not the case now.

In defense of the FBI's HRT, I'm sure they are some of the most skilled members of the FBI. But how can you have a team stationed on the east coast, have a crisis on the west coast, and expect them to gather and deploy in any reasonable time, even if there is no doubt they are capable.

I asked one of the agents what charge they used when breaching an airplane. The agent dismissed my question with a quick, "that's classified." Another team member told me what to use and how to use it. They weren't all self-important bastards. But ask yourself how you can have an elite team and never give them any missions. That blame lies with their administration.

I have lain on the ground and had armed suspects walk by looking for me. I have had a dog sniff my boots while I sat under the bows of a tree, and the owner was holding his leash. In real life operations, you put yourselves in situations where shots could be fired by officers and bad guys. This is not the case in training scenarios in which you know you are going home at night. You have not truly been tested until you are faced with a situation that could cost you or others their life.

//

My first SWAT callout was in Mosier, west of the Dalles. The suspect had been collecting and making hundreds of pounds of explosives. He had set booby traps around his property. Someone broke into his house, and several hundred pounds of explosives were detonated. There were explosives scattered well over a hundred yards. Our assignment as SWAT was to sit on the perimeter all night with night vision to watch for the suspect to return and to keep everyone out of the area.

I had an instant bond with the team members, most of whom were young and whom I had never met.

//

We were called up to serve a search warrant on a biker group near Klamath Falls. It was the middle of winter. There were about ten inches of snow on the ground. Reg Madsen and I walked in about a mile to set up on the rear of the house in the dark. Just before the team executed the warrant, Reg leaned over and said if they bust out of the back and we need to shoot, I want you to take the shot. I said sure, as I thought about it, I wondered why. Reg said, "You are still protected."

I knew what he meant. Reg had just been promoted and was not protected by the troopers Association. I did get a kick out of it. Here we are in a potential shooting situation, and Reg had just realized that he was not part of the protected group anymore.

//

Reg was promoted again later and was not officially part of the team but always stayed in touch with us, and on one operation he came back to assist. Along with all of Reg's other skills, he was good in the water and was scuba rated. We had a group of people who lived in a remote area surrounded by mountains on the back side and a river on the front. When the river was down they could cross on an underwater bridge of sorts, but in the winter when the river was high they used a boat to access the property.

Our team had been watching the property for weeks from a vantage point across the river. From the intel it was decided that we needed to do a river crossing with rafts at a narrow section of the river. It was realized early on that we would need to put team members in the water to cross the river, secure ropes, and pull the rafts across. Since it was winter, the river was high and cold.

Lt. Rick Giestwhite, our SWAT commander contacted Reg and asked if he would assist us with the plan to insert swimmers into the water. Reg selected me and two other team members. After we got the team across, we were to swim downstream and cut their boat loose and secure it to the far side of the river, so the suspects could not cross.

It sounded good on paper. We practiced the river crossing for weeks in ponds. In hindsight it would have been nice to jump in a river and have the swimmers practice too. I had a friend on Portland SWAT who was a SEAL master chief and had intimate knowledge of water operations. I never thought to contact him until after the operation.

We got the entry and perimeter teams safely across the river and started swimming downstream. I was getting old enough that my feet and hands got cold quicker than they would have ten years earlier. We had been in the water twenty minutes in wet suits. I was armed with a knife and pistol. As we reached the boat it took both hands to push the button to open my switch blade knife. We cut the boat free and towed it across the river, and secured it.

We started swimming downstream to our extraction point. The bank was choked with blackberries and underbrush, typical of the Oregon coast. After swimming for several minutes I asked Reg if we were making any headway. He said he didn't think so. We had swum into a current near the bank that was pushing us upstream. We swam out into the main channel and moved down to get extracted.

After-action meetings were conducted on every raid. Since I had no idea what I was doing, I did not question much, however I did realize that my pistol may not have functioned due to the amount of silt in the water.

Our operation was a success Lt. Giestwhite was happy with the execution of the raid plan. Lt. Giestwhite and said he was happy no one was hurt during the operation. I suggested that would hold true as long as no one tried to throw me back into the river. It took me an hour to warm up.

A week later I contacted my bomb-squad counterpart and former seal master chief from Portland Police Bureau. I asked him if he would give me some idea of what we should have done if we ended up in a river again. He asked me a series of questions as follows: Did you have on a life vest? Did you wear a hockey type helmet with IR (infrared) stick attached? Did you have a canteen half full of clean water? I had to answer no to all of them. The vest was for obvious reasons. The hockey helmet was for possible head trauma, and the IR stick was so perimeter team members with night vision could keep track of our movement. The half-full canteen was used to be used for buoyancy and cleaning the weapon when reach your targets. I think these are common-sense suggestions, and I'm not giving up any SEAL secrets. I did write an after-action report to suggest ideas for the future. You can never be too safe.

I think this was the only time we conducted an operation where we had several items that could have assisted us and kept us safer during the operation.

//

The cold was always and issue as a perimeter team member. We were sent into areas to watch the suspect hours before the entry team arrived. After you spend a night in the snow, you learn to reevaluate your gear, but you had to compromise. If you get the warmest boots available you may not be able to hike in them for a mile or move over steep terrain. Needless to say my feet got cold on the early-morning deployments.

//

When the perimeter team deployed early, it meant moving into an area in the dark. If you have not been in the woods with no moon you don't know how dark that is. There were not enough night-vision goggles for everyone. On one operation we had to grab the pack of the man ahead of us because we could not see a thing. As we passed one neighbor up the canyon, a dog came out and was barking within a couple of feet and we could not see him.

Night vision is great, but you lose depth perception. As we dropped off teams into their positions, one of our team members walked off about a four-foot bank. I heard the air come out of him as he landed on his back, but not another sound—no scream and no cussing. He organized himself and moved on.

This was in the Medford area, so the vegetation is quite different from the mountains of Eastern Oregon. When the sun came up some of us realized we had moved into patches of poison oak. Knowing it could be a problem I had rubbed Tecnu on before we deployed. I went directly back to the motel after the operation and showered with all my gear on using more Tecnu to clean everything; I'm sold on that stuff. I was fortunate; some of the guys reacted to exposure to poison oak I did not.

//

During one training cycle at Camp Rilea, we were training in one area and Portland SWAT was training at another area. When you get that many guys working and playing together the pranks start to escalate. On one occasion Portland found an unlocked door to the barracks and then an unlocked room. They attacked one of our SWAT members biting him all over and growling like a pack of dogs.

We couldn't let this go without some retaliation. We decided to target them when they had their bonfire on the beach the last night of training. Since I was the explosives guy, I made up a noise maker to divert their attention while several others approached their campfire to gas them.

We stirred up a hornet's nest; there was an explosion of bodies running in the sand toward the barracks, which were a mile away. There were so many swamps between the beach and the barracks you needed to stay near roads or risk running into the swamps in the dark. It turned out it was every man for himself. You do not want to get caught by a bunch of SWAT guys from another team, especially when they have had a couple of drinks.

By the time I got back, I realized that Portland SWAT could have beaten me back to the barracks; some of them had vehicles near the beach. I decided to stay away from the barracks entrance and snuck into the officers' club. I found three other team members there who had the same idea. We were done with training, but I had a long drive home the next morning. I crashed in the club until the sun came up. Retaliation seemed like a good idea at the time, but it did cost me some sleep. We could not let their attack go without some response.

//

While the state police had a helicopter, we had access to it for SWAT operations. It was nice to have a helicopter to fly us over targets so we could get photographs and the layout of property we were preparing to raid. On raid day they would fly the perimeter. But my favorite way to use the helicopter was as s shooting platform. Since we had the helicopter we used it on operations we needed to practice shooting out of it. Our pilot was very good; he made it easy to stay on target.

//

Sometimes you wonder what people are thinking. BENT wrote a search warrant on a huge methamphetamine operation run by an old man and some local methamphetamine users in Umatilla County. The quantity was great enough that the case was adjudicated in federal court.

The OSP SWAT team was called due to the unpredictable and violent nature of methamphetamine users.

Upon execution of the search warrant, the entry team secured several suspects as they cleared the house. When the team reached the back bedroom, the suspect was standing near his bed. There was a handgun lying near him on the bed. The suspect looked at the team members and dove for the handgun.

The two officers jumped the suspect and secured the handgun. While the entry-team members were relating the facts to me about the arrest, I asked the old man what he was thinking. He just shrugged his shoulders.

No one wants to be put in a situation where they are forced to shoot someone. These two officers used great restraint and risked their lives to save his. The old man had a reminder of the poor decision he made the next time he looked in a mirror.

//

A friend or ours and fellow Detective Mike Durr was working a case near Dayville, where a suspect, Billy, had killed his parents and went on the run. Detective Durr drove up on the suspect who grabbed a high-powered rifle and shot him from about one hundred yards. Detective Durr was severely injured, and Billy took off on foot into the mountainous area near Dayville.

The OSP SWAT and all the detectives in the district arrived to conduct a manhunt. It seemed like no stone was left unturned. There were officers searching barns and outbuildings all over the area.

One of the local deputies and local officers said that there was one ranch that no one had checked, so Detective Randy Crutcher and I went to contact him. Prior to leaving for the ranch we received several warnings from local officers, including OSP fish and wildlife officers, that Mr. Johnson was unstable and had threatened law enforcement officers in the past.

Randy and I arrived at a locked gate with no trespassing signs attached to each side. You could see a tee pee and buildings in the valley. We honked the horn a few times and here came Mr. Johnson on a four-wheeler—he was moving. I thought we would have a confrontation. We told Mr. Johnson that Billy had killed his parents and shot a police officer and that he was on foot in area. We knew Mr. Johnson had several thousand acres were Billy could hide and there were some cabins further up the mountain.

We asked Mr. Johnson if we could look around his place for Billy. Mr. Johnson never hesitated. He said, "I don't want that SOB on my place come on in." Randy and I followed Mr. Johnson down the canyon to his compound. There were overseas cargo containers dug into the mountain, tee pees, and other structures where he was living.

Randy and Mr. Johnson hit it off right away. Somehow it came up that Mr. Johnson was familiar with some interview techniques that Randy had been trained in, so we now had common ground. Mr. Johnson said had been involved in a serious automobile accident that caused a change in his behavior. I was glad he was having a good day.

Mr. Johnson said that he would drive us to his cabins in the upper meadow. He asked me if he could bring a gun. I told Mr. Johnson it was his property, if he wanted to bring a gun it was up to him. I was not quite prepared for what I saw next.

Mr. Johnson went into a building and came out with a rifle and an arm load of ammo. He stopped, went back in, and came out stuffing a handgun into his pants. Mr. Johnson told us his life story as we drove up the mountain. We gave him some tips on how to approach his cabins while crossing open ground, he seemed to be enjoying himself as he helped us clear his cabins. We did not find Billy.

When we got back to his compound he offered to show us around. Mr. Johnson was off the grid. He had solar panels and a bank of batteries feeding power to his underground living quarters. He had taken three cargo containers, welded them together, and dug them into the mountain. He said he had used his dozer to drag a concrete truck up the mountain and poured two feet of concrete over the containers with a couple of skylights. The front of the containers was covered by a glass enclosure that faced south to capture passive solar heat; it was actually quite impressive.

We did not find Billy that day, but it goes to show you that you can never predict how people will react to the presence of law enforcement. Mr. Johnson invited us to bring the wives back and hunt his place. There were deer everywhere. I doubt that Randy took him up on his offer. I know I never went back; there was no sense pushing our luck.

Billy turned himself in the next night. He was cold and hungry. Detective Durr went through a long recovery process but survived his wounds.

THE WORLD ACCORDING TO MIKE

SOME BIG CITY CHIEFS of police are taking a stand for gun control. Gun control laws do not work. We dealt with armed suspects all the time. I mentioned a few cases involving weapons, because there was some other point I was making. Guns were so common that it was a surprise if we did not find guns. The world these guys live in is dangerous. If you compare the effects of gun laws in Chicago to those of Houston, you see many similarities and some amazing differences:

Here is the tale of two cities, as I found it on the internet: (I looked up the Murder rate on neutral news web sites, after I saw the comparison and found it to be accurate.)

	Chicago, IL	Houston, TX
Population	2.7 million	2.15 million
Median HH income	$38,600	$37,000
Percentage African American	32.9 percent	24 percent
Percentage Hispanic	28.9 percent	44 percent
Percentage Asian	5.5 percent	6 percent
Percentage non-Hispanic or White	31.7 percent	26 percent

A reasonably similar matchup—until you look at this:

	Chicago, IL	Houston, TX
Concealed carry gun law	No	Yes
Number of gun stores	0	84 dedicated gun stores; 1,500 places to buy guns
Homicides, 2012	506	217
Homicides per 100,000 people	18.4	10

We dealt with armed suspects all the time. That said I am not in favor of any kind of gun control. We need to enforce the laws we already have. Bad guys will always have guns. The only thing gun control will do is take guns away from honest people. If the government tries to take away any gun from me I will not comply; they will have turned an honest citizen into a criminal.

The majority of the weapons we seized (and we seized thousands over my career) were either stolen; obtained through a straw purchase (where someone else buys the gun for you); or retained after the owner became a felon.

Gun control could prevent you from protecting your family. There are not enough police officers to watch all of us all the time, especially those of us who choose to live in rural areas. My favorite bumper sticker reads, "If guns kill people, do pencils misspell words?" Guns are not inherently evil; they can't react without human intervention.

Enforce the laws we have; lock up bad guys; and make criminals think twice. The criminals need to believe the person they are attacking is armed. You are not helping out law enforcement by banning guns. As police we always plan and prepare for the worst case scenario; we treat everyone as if they are armed.

If you are one of these people who need to worry about everything, don't worry that your neighbor has a gun. I think we are in more danger from the liberal media. Due to the nature of my assignments, we received a lot of press. Even if we wrote the details on our news log the media always seemed to get something wrong. I rarely believe what I hear on the news or read in the paper. Even when most of the facts right, they leave our details or slant the article to fit their agenda.

I think the liberal media is one of the most divisive institutions in America, they insight riots and violent protests. Consider what happened after the Rodney King arrest: night after night the liberal media showed a short clip of police attacking a poor, defenseless man. Come on, I've thrown worse beatings to suspects than that and I was following department policy too.

I have talked to LAPD officers who told me they were directed not to fight suspects on PCP. They were instructed to use nightsticks until the suspect complied. If they thought Rodney King was on PCP, they had every right to strike him until he complied. If you were not there, don't pass judgment. The media never showed Rodney King's initial attack on the police.

For another example, look at the hate generated by the media after the Trayvon Martin shooting. For a month the press reported that George Zimmerman did not have any visible wounds. When the trial started and evidence was revealed the photographs told a different story. Mr. Zimmerman had what looked like a broken nose and lacerations all over the back of his head. I did not see any retractions—only more attacks.

These types of incidents directly affect our police. Whether they are warranted or not, people looked at the police with mistrust after days of hearing how incompetent the police were.

JUST SHUT UP

On the subject of shootings or other incidents involving violence, I am sick and tired of hearing, "if I had been there I would have done this," or "I would have done that." I will call bullshit right now. No police officer will see the same incident the same way another police officer does, let alone how a civilian will. Based on training and experience, they will see or perceive the incident differently.

Cops are as guilty as the untrained, inexperienced civilian about forming an opinion without knowing all the facts and circumstances. Every shooting I have been involved in or witnessed seems to have one thing in common: the cops who show up always have an opinion about what happened and how it would have turned out if they had been there. God love them; I know they mean well, but they should just shut up. No one can know what he or she would have done.

Civilians who read about an incident in the paper suddenly have an opinion about what happened, even though they have no training or experience. It is easy to sit in the recliner and Monday-morning-quarterback something they are reading in the paper. Do not be misled; what you read in the paper is rarely accurate or complete. I am telling you from years of typing up press releases after an incident. I rarely recognized the story of an incident I was involved in by the time it was regurgitated by a member of the press.

Police are the worst critics of themselves. I have heard so many officers say something to the effect that if they had just done this or that, maybe things would have turned out differently. The truth is that most violent suspects dictate the behavior of the responding officer. Now we believe that the outcome will turn out differently depending on the officer who arrives. The job of the responding officer who arrives at a violent incident is officially to stop the threat. You could stop the threat of violence by your presence and demeanor, or you could be forced to take the suspect's life.

Here is a situation where mitigating factors are involved, let's say that a one-hundred-pound female officer arrives at the scene of a violent assault. She may realize that she is not physically capable of stopping the assault by laying hands on the suspect. She is forced to draw her weapon and demands the suspect stop beating the victim. If she realizes the suspect will kill the victim unless she reacts, she may be forced to shoot the suspect. In the same scenario if a 220-pound male officer who is trained in mixed martial arts arrives on the scene, he will evaluate the situation differently and may feel he is capable of physically taking the suspect into custody. Neither response is right or wrong; but both responses should be judged from the totality of the circumstances at the time. That includes the physical stature of the officer who responded to the scene.

Don't miss the point of what I am saying just because I used an illustration of a slightly built female officer versus a 220-pound male officer, who are both physically fit. You could plug in any two officers; let's say the first officer to arrive is old and out of shape. He may be forced to make the same decision the female officer made. My point is that no two situations will play out the same, even if the general circumstances seem identical.

I was present when four officers were facing the same threat of violence, knowing the same background information regarding the suspect. I shot the suspect; the other three officers knew that was the right decision but did not shoot. Since I was the senior officer, had received hundreds more hours of training, and was SWAT trained, they may have been deferring to me to make the decision. Again, everything needs to be taken into account. Please don't feel I am making a judgment about these officers, because I am not. They are some of my best friends, and I trusted them with my life before and after the incident. On that day I was quicker on the trigger.

OFF-DUTY ADVENTURES

My wife was listening when Dr. Kevin Gilmartin conducted a stress seminar in Pendleton. OSP hired Dr. Gilmartin to travel to OSP offices around the state to talk to our wives so that they would have some insight into police behavior. Dr. Gilmartin talked about the "arsenic hour," which was no more than giving their husbands some space for an hour after they get home. The idea is you let them relax before you throw more crises at them when they get home.

Dr. Gilmartin was a former police officer who understood the stress and the emotional roller coaster that accompanied police work. Dr. Gilmartin was able to convey the necessity for police officers to be involved in activities to relieve stress.

Shari always encouraged me to take time with the boys. There was a loose-knit group of state, city, and county law enforcement officers; local business men; and an occasional attorney that took one week per year together to relax on a guys' vacation.

We made several trips with Howard Gipe, a sergeant with the Montana Highway Patrol and eventual county commissioner of Flat Head County. Howard guided several fifty- to seventy-five-mile loops into the Bob Marshal Wilderness. These were trips that none of us could have afforded to take if we had to pay for them.

Later on we took road trips on motorcycles with up to fifteen riders and a support driver in our group. We made loops into Canada, Whidbey Island, Montana, Wyoming, Sturgis, Oregon Coast Highway, and Laguna Seca Raceway in California. Someone in our group would take turns planning the route we would take.

We also took trips to Moab, Utah to ride dirt bikes and four-wheelers through the desert. These trips were also taken by roughly the same loose-knit group. After a shooting I was involved in, we heard the lieutenant had told headquarters the usual suspects were involved in the shooting. He was right; the group I played with was also the core group I worked with.

My dad and I were very close. We always took time to hunt together and to spend time at the family cabin. We were very successful hunters, but the taking of a deer or elk was the bonus. We always planned to take a trip to moose hunt in Alaska. My dad died at the age of sixty-two from an aggressive form of cancer. His early passing probably took more of a toll on me than I thought at the time. I know I had a few outbursts of anger that were probably detrimental to the health of whoever was in my path at the time.

A good friend of mine, Dale Freemen, was the head wrestling coach at Pendleton High School. He had the trust in me to allow me to be an assistant coach for twenty years. This was a great chance for me to be directly involved with some very motivated young men at a time when I had lost faith in society and our youth. Dale was a very successful coach who was able to take the team on yearly trips to places like Las Vegas and Ketchikan, Alaska. Ketchikan is where one of my biggest adventures began. Dale's cousin Chuck lived near Ketchikan, so he came to visit us while we were wrestling at Ketchikan High School.

Chuck relayed several stories of hunting moose while floating the Yukon River and its tributaries. Mike Loughary, who was my partner on the narcotics task force, was also an assistant wrestling coach at Pendleton High School and went on the Ketchikan wrestling trip. We told Chuck to let us know if he ever needed hunting partners, and we would gladly tag along.

About two years later I received a call from Chuck; I had almost forgotten about him. Chuck said he had blown up a boat motor the year before and needed $2,000 to replace it. Chuck said if Mike Loughary and I still wanted to hunt, he would take us for $1,000 a piece to offset the charges to replace the motor. I mentioned it to Shari, who said that this is a trip I had always wanted to take with my dad and that I may never have another chance. I called Mike Loughary who was on board as well. Our Alaska adventure was only a couple of months off.

During our planning phase, Chuck told me that we were going to be hunting near Ruby, in the Nowitna drainage. Chuck said his boat was in Galena, which was about fifty miles down the Yukon River. We scheduled our flight to land in Galena to meet Chuck and his hunting partner.

A week later I got a call from Chuck who wanted me to come a week early to help him float two skiffs, three hundred miles downriver from Nenana on the Tanana River to the Yukon River down to Galena. I could not get that much time off, so I declined. Chuck made the trip with one canoe and a row boat lashed to each other; one boat held our supplies.

The day finally came, Mike and I arrived at the Galena airport, Chuck was there to meet us. We also met Ray who was a logger from Oregon. Mike and I were transported to the river and an awaiting boat. It was a twenty-four-foot aluminum boat with a cabin. We were assigned the task of putting the two skiffs on top of the boat; as we were securing the skiffs we were confronted by several Native Alaskans who were upset that we had not settled our debt before taking the boat. Mike and I explained that we had just landed and had no idea what deal they had struck with Chuck. After quite some time Chuck arrived and left with the leader of the group; when Chuck returned we were free to go.

We had two fifty-five-gallon drums of gas in the front of the boat as we headed down the Yukon River. Out of confusion I asked Chuck where we were going, because he had told us we were going upriver to Ruby and then up the Nowitna drainage. Chuck said they had always wanted to hunt the slough (river) where the Iditarod flows into the Innoko Slough. This was over three hundred miles from where I told Shari where we would be and over two hundred and fifty miles from Galena. Chuck assured us that he had a buddy in a float plane who would check on us.

We left about three hours before dark, and about an hour after we left Galena, the motor quit. Chuck and Ray were handy guys. They determined that the fuel pump had quit, so we ran a hose from one of the fifty-five-gallon drum directly to the engine, and we were off. We camped on the beach that evening.

The next day we headed downriver, getting stuck along the way on sand bars in the middle of the Yukon. Mike and I decided that we would handle the fifty-five-gallon drums of gas. Chuck and Ray smoked and went out there a couple of times with lit cigarettes to check fuel levels.

On the third day we hit the mouth of the north fork of the Innoko Slough. Slough is an accurate description of a river that winded like a snake and had no current. In the afternoon we hit the main Innoko River, and it got wider and straighter. There is no dry land in this drainage, and the banks are littered with willows and bogs. About thirty-five miles up the main Innoko we hit the mouth of the Iditarod River, about a half mile past the Iditarod River the engine seized. Chuck looked at Ray and asked if he had added the two-cycle oil to the engine. Ray said, "I thought you added it." I realized that two years in a row these two had burnt up an engine by not adding two cycle oil. We drifted slowly back down stream. Just south of the Iditarod River was a thirty-foot-wide beach above the river. We tied off and were warned by Chuck to keep an eye out for the changing depth of the river; we did not want the boat to be high and dry on the bank.

While Chuck and Ray tore the engine apart, Mike and I decided to take a skiff and explore the area. We had a twelve-foot canoe and a twelve-foot skiff with six-horse motors for each to hunt with. Mike and I claimed the skiff. We found a bull moose on the bank about half mile from camp. He was right at the forty-five inch minimum for us to shoot and it was the first day of our hunt.

When we got back to camp, Chuck told us that they had gotten some WD-40 into the cylinders, and they were able to free the piston, but the motor could only idle without blowing apart. There was no walking out of the area we were in; you could not walk down the beach, and every creek crossing was like quicksand.

We drew numbers for first shooter so there was some level of discipline if a bull moose appeared and we were all there. Mike drew number one shooter; Chuck drew number two shooter, and I drew number three. Since we split up to hunt Mike got first shot in our boat and Chuck got first shot in his boat.

Mike and I decided we had come to hunt, so we set up our tent and planned our hunt for the next day. We saw several decent bulls and lots of bear and wolf tracks everywhere we beached the boat to look for moose. We never made it more than a hundred yards from the bank of the river, due to the amount of water and brush. I had brought two hand held radios that had about a 6 mile range, I gave Chuck and Ray one of them. This was the only radio we had; Mark did not have a satellite phone or a survival beacon. But I figured in a couple of days his buddy would fly in to check on us, so we could tell him we had engine trouble.

On the evening of the sixth day we were seeing a lot of moose; Chuck and Ray were about five miles above us on the Iditarod Slough. This was the snakiest river I had ever seen; it was one turn after another. We heard a faint call from Chuck asking for help getting a moose cut up. It was about two hours before dark, and we were about eight miles from camp. Mike and I headed up the slough.

When we arrived we found Chuck and Ray standing over a fifty-nine-inch moose. The celebrating was short lived as we started the big task of cutting up the moose. As it got dark we were loading meat into the boats so we could get back to camp; we could see a storm coming. As we were ready to push off, Ray approached us with the head. I told him no way we were taking anything else. We had very little free board in our boat. I could see Chuck and Ray were pissed off, but we could not take any more weight safely.

It was getting dark and windy, and the rain was coming hard. Within a half hour, Mike and I could not see each other in our boat. I could hear the motor on Chuck and Ray's boat as we rounded each corner. When it got black, I knew I had to turn the boat, because we were about to hit the bank. As we came around a corner about three miles from camp, I could not hear Chuck and Ray's motor. Mike turned on his spotlight, and we could see Chuck and Ray in the water. They were struggling to get to shore, so they dragged the boat near the bank. Mike and I hit the beach and helped them drag the boat loaded with meat out of the water. Chuck and Ray had also saved their gear and rifles.

As wet as they were they jerked the motor off the boat and attempted to get it started. They got the spark plug out and started draining water from the engine. There was no way to build a fire, there was no driftwood in the area and all the willows were green and wet. While Chuck and Ray worked on the engine, Mike and I unloaded the meat onto a tarp on the beach. Chuck got the engine going and headed for camp with an empty boat.

Mike and I headed to camp hugging the left bank so we were close to shore, since we had to make a left turn at the Innoko River to find camp. It took about an hour to find camp, due to the fact we were barley moving.

The next morning when I stepped out of the tent, I stepped into water. The Innoko River was rising because of the amount of rain we were getting. We decided we needed to start heading for civilization, since it was going to take a long time to get back with the crippled motor. But, first we needed to take the big boat upriver to retrieve the rest of the meat. Mike Stayed to pack up our camp while we headed up the slough, towing the canoe. When we arrived at the crash site, Chuck and Ray tried to take the canoe to shore to get the meat. The storm was raging, and I could not hold the boat in place with no power. I almost ran over them. We finally ran the boat up on the beach to retrieve the meat. I prayed we could push it off once we got the meat aboard. After pushing off the beach, we headed back to pick up Mike.

Everyone was on edge as we headed down the Innoko River. I kept my rifle and ammo close; Mike had packed his away in frustration. As luck would have it, just before dark we came around a corner, and there was a nice bull moose. There was little time to waste. I told Mike he was up, he could not find his ammo. I stepped out and shot the Bull as we drifted past. I had a bull moose on the ground; I had gotten a very nice sixty-two-and-a-half-inch trophy. (Sorry, Mike).

We beached the boat and started taking pictures and cutting up our bull. Without warning we heard a "woof" and some crashing. I did not look back; I knew a bear was coming. I stuck my knife in the moose and ran for my rifle, which I had left on the boat. Chuck was close and started shooting into the brush. Chuck stood guard behind us as we finished cutting up the meat. As we moved the meat to the boat Mike and I realized there was not much room on the boat. We had to sleep on the beach with a bear in the area. Chuck and Ray slept on the boat; Mike and I slept little, and I kept my .44 Mag on my chest.

By noon the next day we reached the north fork of the Innoko River and stopped for a quick bath. The water was cold, and the black flies ate us alive. We camped about halfway up the north fork that evening. We relaxed and ate moose for dinner. While we were in camp, a boat passed going down stream. This was the first time we had seen people since we left the Yukon River.

By noon the next day we arrived at the Yukon River—it was the moment of truth. We would have to give the engine enough gas to push us against the river's seven mile-per-hour current. We eased into the current, and Chuck pushed us upstream. I used my GPS and figured out we were reaching a max speed of seven miles per hour. Mike and I looked at our gas reserves, and I looked up how far we were away from Kaltag, which was over 110 miles away. There was no way we could reach Galena with the amount of fuel we had. If you look at a map, there is no place to get gas or anything else between the north fork of the Innoko Slough and Kaltag.

That night at camp we all realized we were in trouble. Chuck knew winter was coming and the last tug and barge would be in Kaltag. We hoped to arrive and get a ride on the tug to Galena, where Mike and I could catch a plane back to Fairbanks. Chuck and Ray planned to use the tug to get their boat back to civilization.

The next day we knew we were going to run out of gas before we could reach Kaltag. Chuck said we will just go until we run out of fuel. I threw a fit. I told him to beach the boat so we did not end up adrift on a sandbar. We were having breakfast in the cab of the boat using a lantern for light and a propane stove to cook. After breakfast I unscrewed the propane bottle to put it away, when a brass washer from the stove got stuck in the propane bottle. The gas started filling the cabin. With the lantern running I knew it would not be long before we had a fire; I opened the back window and threw it out. Mark and Chuck were mad, but as I saw the bottle spinning in circles in the Yukon I knew I had done the right thing.

Around noon we were running on fumes, so we talked Chuck into beaching the boat on the west bank. As it turned out we were on Quail Island. It was dry, and there was a lot of wood. As we came to shore we stripped the wires out of the depth finder. We had to fix the problem before we left, or we would be stuck on a sandbar in the middle of the Yukon River with no power to get off.

Chuck said he would take the canoe and head to Kaltag with a fifty-five-gallon barrel and get more gas for the boat. Chuck was just out of sight in a bend in the river, when we heard his motor sputter and die. Chuck drifted back and said the motor they had sunk had given out. We put our last motor on the canoe, and Chuck was on his way.

We decided to work on the depth finder in the morning. We were still over thirty miles from Kaltag, so we knew we would not see Chuck for quite some time.

The next morning I put on my waders and was working on the wiring when we heard a boat coming down stream. We waved and a boat full of Native Alaskans came to see what was up. We told them we were out of fuel and asked if they could spare some, they agreed on a price of forty dollars and moose ribs for five gallons of fuel. It was a great deal. While we were explaining our situation, Ray told our guests that Indians had stolen gas from us while we were hunting. Before I could choke him out the oldest Indian woman asked if we had seen Indians steal the gas. I cut him off and told her no one had stolen gas; Chuck and Ray had not brought enough for the distance we had covered. That comment could have cost us the fuel if they had not been so kind as to have overlooked Ray's foolishness.

Late that afternoon Chuck arrived with some gas, and we had completed the repair on the depth finder, so we put the gas in the boat and headed upriver. As darkness approached we were again running out of gas. We rounded a bend in the river and saw the lights of Kaltag, but we knew we could not make it there. There happened to be a couple of cabins near the river, so we pulled over.

I claimed a bed; I needed some sleep badly. We built a huge fire on the bank of the river. About an hour later we could hear a boat coming. A Native Alaskan arrived to see what was going on, because he owned the cabins. He asked if we had gone into the cabins. Before I could say yes our buddy Ray said no. I told him we had, and I was willing to pay to stay the night. He allowed us to use the cabin at no charge. He agreed to send someone with gas in the morning.

We knew our new friend had been drinking. I hoped he would remember to send someone. After he took off we heard him hit a log, which we saw a lot of in the river. My first thought was that he had been ejected from his boat, because the motor had died. About a minute later we heard the motor start; he gave it full throttle and headed toward the village in the dark.

As promised early the next morning a Kaltag native arrived with enough gas for us to make it to the village. We were lucky as the last tug of the year was there off-loading a barge full of supplies. We talked to the tug boat captain, who agreed to tie Chuck's boat to the tug and tow us upstream at least as far as Galena, so Mike and I could catch a plane. We gave the captain a couple of hind quarters of the moose for his trouble. It was a small price to pay.

We left that afternoon and traveled all night. We were able to shower on the tug, and they fed us dinner. By about daylight we were in Galena. Chuck was convinced that he and Ray could make it the rest of the way on their own if they took it easy. We went through the moose meat that had been rained on for days; we had rotated it as often as we could, but it was spoiling. We had to throw some of it off the boat before Chuck and Ray set us on the beach at Galena. We agreed to meet them in a few days at Chuck's place in Fairbanks.

We found a local from Galena to drive us to the airport. I was unsure if we would ever see our hunting partners again.

The boat did break down again, but to Chuck and Ray's credit, they out with the boat and my moose rack. Would I go hunt with them again? Hell yes it was an adventure, but I would have a rescue beacon and a satellite phone. And I would offer to monitor the two-cycle oil for the engine. Alaskans are wired differently; they don't sweat the small stuff. Chuck is a survivor, and I want to thank him for the adventure.

STAYING GROUNDED

I HAVE TO THANK a couple of people outside of my family and law enforcement for keeping me grounded. In law enforcement it is easy to see everyone we deal with as an asshole. If you don't have a life outside of law enforcement, soon everyone is an asshole.

A couple of friends took my family and me into their inner circle and helped keep me grounded. They didn't keep me entirely from becoming cynical, but I could have been worse.

First I want to thank Bill Umbarger, my longtime friend and neighbor. He is a good Christian soul who never judged me and was always there to help. As much as I was gone, it was reassuring to have a neighbor who was there to watch over my family.

The Umbarger clan accepted my family into their family; I spent a lot of my off duty time with them either hunting or working cows. I could leave work, come home, and be in a totally different world. It seemed like everyone I contacted was a parasite sucking the life out of our community. When I'd hang around with the Umbargers, I knew that what I did for a living was important for our community.

I want to thank Dale Freeman. I met Dale through the Pendleton High School wrestling program. Dale was a good friend who trusted me with many young lives. I enjoyed the many hours I spent with Dale and Pendleton's finest young men and women.

If I had not been involved with these young people, I could have gotten trapped in a world that seemed like there was no hope for any of them. At work I ran into kids who were second- and third-generation freeloaders; these kids did not have a prayer. Their parents were drug users and deadbeats, and there were no positive role models in their lives.

I remember talking to one young man who had a bright future in college athletics. I asked him where he was thinking of going to college. He said, "I don't have to go to college, my grandma said the government would take care of me." And it did; we did not win them all over.

Dale had some hard-luck kids in the wrestling room, but we had a chance to show them if they worked hard, they could accomplish their goals.

REFLECTION

I LOOK BACK ON my career and realize how many great opportunities I had. I received some of the best training available in our country; I attended several national training facilities. We had some of the best tactical officers in the country work and train with us. With the budget problems in the state of Oregon I can't imagine how anyone else will ever be able to attend more quality training than I received.

I was a tactical sponge; I soaked up as much training as I could. I was fortunate enough on several occasions to train and relax with Chuck Mawhinney, who is one of the most decorated Marine Corps snipers in our country. Chuck had 103 confirmed and 226 probable kills in Vietnam; his story was not known for years. Chuck received numerous commendations including the Bronze Star for Combat and a Purple Heart. Chuck's rifle is now retired in the Marine Corps Museum at Quantico, Virginia. Chuck volunteered his time to hang out with our SWAT team when we trained in Baker City, Oregon. I will forever be grateful for the time I was able to spend with him. Chuck Mawhinney was all about going back to the basics of rifle-shooting. I know he made me a better shooter.

I thought about Chuck Mawhinney and others I had talked to over the years while on an operation at Tollgate in the Blue Mountains. We were watching an armed suspect who was dealing methamphetamine in a remote area. I snuck in near his trailer, so I could keep an eye on him while the rest of the team watched other suspects. This was a daytime operation, so I crawled under a fir tree that had grown to the ground.

I could see the suspect who seemed nervous and was walking the area with his German shepherd. At one point the suspect came to the dog, who was growling and looking right at me. As they approached I thought about Chuck Mawhinney lying in the jungle, undetected while the enemy passed. I stayed motionless as the dog came up and sniffed my boots. The suspect finally hollered at his dog and called him off.

Just knowing that others have been in similar situations and survived is sometimes all the edge you need in order to have the confidence to accomplish your mission. I think it is important to acknowledge how important training is for law enforcement officers. I worry about the quality of training they are receiving every time I hear about budget cuts.

My dad asked several times why I did not go up for promotion. He told me, "You are not just responsible for Mike anymore. You need to think about Shari and the kids." In his eyes I was volunteering for the most dangerous tasks for my own gratification. He was probably right. I told him the state police would not promote you in the same office where you work, which was true at the time. So I would have to uproot the family and leave my hobby farm if I wanted a promotion.

I knew sergeants and lieutenants who had lost their houses due to promotion and transfer. Sergeants also made less money than troopers working overtime. I did look into it at one point; the first year I would have lost $13,000. So the type of guys going up for rank were ego maniacs who wanted rank at any cost, be it familial or financial. It was easier for a single guy who did not have a wife working or kids in school; or guys who wanted to climb the ladder as high as it took them, so going up for sergeant was a stepping stone they would endure.

Truth be told, I had a hard time working a case up, doing a raid plan, and sending someone into the line of fire to complete my task. If I did my job right, my raid plan should allow me to complete the task unharmed. I had as much or more training than anyone in our department at raid planning and execution. I was the point man on hundreds of raids we conducted with our entry team, and I was always comfortable there.

I read somewhere where that a politician [administrator] is someone who will risk *your* life to defend *our* country. I could not have lived with myself if I had drawn up a plan that sent a young man into a situation where I made a miscalculation of the circumstances that had gotten him killed. I was better served to lead a charge and count on my training and experience to make up for any lack of planning.

After my dad died I did go through the promotion process and passed the assessment center testing. I ended up on the promotion list for sergeant, where I stayed until I retired. I was asked if I would take a couple of jobs that came up, but I really had no intention of taking a sergeant position. I think I went through the process for my ego or to prove to myself that had I wanted to move up in rank I could have.

When I retired from the Oregon State Police I was a dinosaur—someone who was about to over stay his welcome. I think headquarters was glad to see me go. I had a retired superintendent tell me that he lost some sleep, wondering if I was going to get in trouble and end up standing tall in front of his desk. I told him I never worried about him doing the right thing. We had been around each other enough over the years that both of us had revealing stories about each other that I did not mentioned here and never will.

RETIREMENT

I HAVE TALKED TO officers who are eligible to retire but have reservations about leaving. I hear what they are saying, but I don't understand. I knew I would retire when I turned fifty. I had twenty-eight years on the job, and that was enough. I had no idea what I would do, but I knew I would not stay. I never looked back and wished I had stayed. I wanted to get out and enjoy a normal life, whatever that is.

I guess I look at things from a different perspective; I was fortunate to do every job I ever wanted to do in law enforcement. I had success, and I had the respect of my peers. I did not think I was irreplaceable. I was fully aware that when I walked away I would be replaced by a younger and probably smarter detective. Granted he or she will do the job differently than I did. But that does not make it better or worse, just different.

I was a liability to the Oregon State Police. I did not like change, and everything was changing. I got away with a lot more than the younger detectives, because I knew the system. I could rough up suspects that needed a tune up, and they did not complain, because I was treating them the way they knew they deserved to be treated. In hind sight, my attitude may have been a bad example for young detectives.

Think about this: how many fifty-year-old guys are in good enough shape to come to your rescue in a physical confrontation? Not many. I could still handle myself when I was fifty, because I was a little meaner than most, and I always struck first. Nowadays the police have more tools at their disposal. When I started, we had night sticks and guns. If I had stayed around maybe I could have learned to use a stun gun to shock people into submission, which may have been entertaining.

After I left the state police I built a new home. During the building process I realized I had a few skills. I could pour concrete, lay stone, and do tile work; I could frame a structure and do my own electrical, so I turned that into a second career. I don't know how contractors last as long as they do. I lasted eight years before it wore me out.

I have been lucky enough to make friends with local land owners who trust me to hunt predators on their property. Cougar, bears, wolves, and coyotes are a real problem for ranchers who run cattle in the mountains.

Predator hunting gives me the occasional adrenaline rush I need to stay focused. When someone tells you they are going predator hunting, you probably think they are talking about hunting coyotes or bobcat. When I am calling for predators, I give the coyotes a pass.

The first time I set up to call a cougar, I shot a very large tom. I was hooked. As much as I was using the call, I learned I could call cougar, bears, and wolves with the same sequence of calls. The only down side was that every time I set up to call, I had to be aware that a cougar, bear, or wolf may be coming. I have had all three species sneak into within thirty yards of me before I saw them.

I have learned to set the call farther away from me. Even though I am more careful now I have had to shoot two charging bear. Both bear knew I was there, because I was yelling at them.

Last fall I stopped at one of the ranches and told the owner I was headed up to call bears. He decided he wanted to come along. That morning we saw three bears and two of them came running to the call. My friend grew up where we were calling, so he knew there were a lot of bears around, but I think that experience surprised him a little.

Last spring a friend from church called and said he had drawn a spring bear tag and wanted to know if I would try to call a bear for him. We went to the mountains the next evening. I had him sit on a ridge on an old skid road, where I had seen a bear. I set the call about forty yards from him on the skid road, and I moved down the ridge so I could watch his back.

After we both got settled in, I turned the call on. It was less than five minutes later that I saw a cougar running out of the canyon on the skid road toward my friend. I could not get a shot because he was too far back on the road, and I could only see the top of his shoulder. The cougar must have seen my buddy move because he ran right past the call, into a small opening. I was able to get off two shots, but the cougar did not slow down.

I started yelling to my friend that he had one coming hard. The cougar disappeared from my sight but I knew my friend had seen it, because his elbows and legs were flying. He got to his feet as I was running up the mountain, the cougar died about ten yards from him. I had hit the cougar with both shots, but he went another thirty yards. My friend probably got a better adrenaline rush than I did that day.

I spend my days wandering around in the Blue Mountains of Eastern Oregon and Washington, trying to provide a little security for my friends and get a little exercise for myself.

I would not change a thing I did to get where I am today. Yes, I'm more cynical, and I have less sympathy toward people than the average person. Keep in mind every experience we have in life defines who we are, and we are products of those experiences. I make no excuses for myself or my fellow officers. Just try to remember the next time you hear a story about an incident involving a police officer, that we are coming from a different place and *you were not there*!

CAREER

1975   Joined the Marine Corps; received an Honorable Discharge in 1977
1977   Joined the Oregon State Police; retired in August 2004.

Professional Milestones:

- Patrol Officer (1977–1982)
- Criminal Division (1982–2004)
- In 1983 I started the District IV Explosive Disposal Unit; I retired from that unit with twenty-one years of service.
- In 1985 I helped establish the Blue Mountain Enforcement Narcotics Unit. By 1990 I was a team leader in charge of a six-man unit.
- I worked closely with federal agencies on numerous Organized Crime Drug Enforcement Task Force (OCDETF) cases, all met with the successful prosecution of the targeted suspects.
- In 1996 I was selected to be a member of the Oregon State Police SWAT team. I was assigned to a counter-sniper position. I was also one of the officers assigned to develop risk analysis and tactical response plans until I retired in July 2001; I was an explosive breacher until I retired.
- I helped developed site survey plans for the Bonneville Power Administration, state agencies, and county agencies in Oregon.

These surveys were for tactical response to potential hostage situations or terrorist attacks.

Training:

I received over 4,300 hours of specialized training including:

- Explosives School, FBI certification for Hazardous Device School, and refresher courses for Weapons of Mass Destruction (1997–2001)
- Arson Investigations, National Fire Academy, Emmitsburg, MD (1990)
- Explosive Breaching Gunsite Training Center, Prescott, AZ (1997)
- Advanced Weapons and Tactics, SEAL Team 2, Sixth Army Group, and Oregon State Police SWAT Camp Rilea (1996–2001)

Awards:

- 1988, Peace Officer of the Year Award
- 1989 and 2001, the Oregon Narcotics Officer of the Year Award
- 2001, Medal of Valor, Oregon Peace Officers Association.

CPSIA information can be obtained at www.ICGtesting.com
Printed in the USA
BVOW05s1628251114

376676BV00002B/11/P